Ekphrastia
Gone **WILD**

poems inspired by art

edited by **RICK LUPERT**

Ekphrastia Gone **WILD**

Ain't Got No Press

Design and Layout ~ Rick Lupert

(818) 305-4457

or

15522 Stagg Street
Van Nuys, CA 91406

or

agnp@PoetrySuperHighway.com

or

PoetrySuperHighway.com/agnp

First Edition ~ July, 2013

ISBN: 978-0-9820584-6-6 $15.00

CONTENTS

INTRODUCTION:

In the Springfield Museums in Springfield, Massachusetts, there is a painting called "A Japanese Corner," painted in 1898 by John Haberle. The artist painted the words "Do Not Touch" on a note hanging in the artwork. While regarding the objects in the work, sometime during the summer of 2012, flowers on a small square table, part of a shoji screen with cloths draped over it, a doll which looked like it had fallen on the floor, plus the sign "Do Not Touch," it occurred to me this was a two way experience...a third dimension. Was the artist aware this would hang in a museum and wanted to be sure no-one touched the painting? Was he trying to save the gallery from hiring a docent to stand in the corner to give people the same message? Suffice it to say I didn't touch the painting; but I began to contemplate the act of looking at art as art itself. *Ekphrastia Gone Wild* was born!

I believe that all forms of art come from the same idea. A single idea that comes to the artist may come out in the form of a painting, a poem, a sculpture, or a film. But, no matter the form, it's the same idea. The relationship between an ekphrastic poem and its subject, the original artwork, has the potential to be more of a recreation of that artwork itself, perhaps more so than just an interpretation of it. When I stood in front of "A Japanese Corner" I was part of the painting...*not* touching it just as instructed. Someone else standing by could have viewed me and the painting as one piece.

Equally so the experience of being in front of a work of art is an ekphrastic experience itself. If you're drawn into the painting you might see things which the original artist didn't choose to reveal; But you know they're there. What's hidden behind the tree? Why is she smiling? How does the application of your modern sensibility relate to the ancient scene? All of this expands the original artwork. It becomes part of its family. It creates a dialogue, a bloodline a work of art beyond the natural definition of what art is.

Take the implication in Gene Grabiner's *Winged Victory*, written after viewing the ancient sculpture of Nike...Nike having no idea her name would become owned by a sneaker corporation. Or the eternality of the world Wislawa Szymborska teaches us we've earned in her poem

Vermeer after viewing Vermeer's painting *The Milkmaid*.

Perhaps it's revealed in Ellaraine Lockie's struggle to see what Paul Klee implied he was painting in *untitled*. Or in Mick Moss's attempt to view the 1977 Tate Modern Dada exhibit in his poem *Dada Dada Boo Boo*, only to be shut down by an outfit. Or maybe it's in Brendan Constantine's epic ekphrastic response to an entire evening's worth of artistic output from a variety of mediums in his *I, Meaning You*.

Ekphrastia Gone Wild begs you to never ask the question *What is art*, and assume everything is. Try it the next time you're at the grocery store staring at a sea of tomatoes. Try it while watching the news or passing by a mailbox. There is art everywhere and your every breath as an ekphrastic statement that commingles with it.

So delve in. Bring your third eye or leave it at home. You are about to experience art, this time in the form of words written in response to those singular creative ideas, exploded out of pens, paintbrushes and rolls of film. Perhaps you will *ekphrastize* something in response to all of this. Consider it an exercise. Go.

Let's get wild.

Rick Lupert
July, 2013

*"Painting is poetry that is seen rather than felt,
and poetry is painting that is felt rather than seen."*

Leonardo Da Vinci

*"No great artist ever sees things as they really are.
If he did, he would cease to be an artist."*

Oscar Wilde

*"I am for an art that is political-erotical-mystical, that
does something other than sit on its ass in a museum."*

Claes Oldenburg

Obsession | *Consuelo Marshall*

Crane with deer antler, bronze, 450 B.C.,
Symbols of Power, Masterpieces from the Nanjing Museum

A friend give me his book on "Invasion of the Body Snatchers" and as I read it, I realized he has lived in that movie since he was ten. For fifty years, he has rewound each scene in his head- over and over.

A photo of a crane with an elongated neck and antlers sprouting from an un-birdlike head, has a similar effect on me. I want to go back, 2,400 years to the Zeng Kingdom in China, talk to the artist who created this mixture of deer and crane. Hear how they mixed the symbols of luck and good fortune to form this unearthly creature.

Really, I tell myself, my friend and I have not totally lost our minds, we just let our hearts lead us towards the imagined.

Janus | *Iris Dan*

Bust, Vatican

Standing on the threshold
Janus Bifrons
the two-faced god

One face they say
is turned to the past
the other to the future

I think
he's the child
who cannot grow up

Half of him wants
to run away from home
the other to run back

He will do neither
he's sentenced to stand
forever on the threshold

Winged Victory | *Gene Grabiner*

Nike of Samothrace, unknown sculptor, circa 190 B.C.E.

Before *nike©*
there was
Nike,
only one Winged Victory. Now,
of 13 googled pages, Nike is on page 13,
after shoe upon shoe,
swoosh© and swoosh©, and
Tiger©.
Winged Victory—lost to shoes?
From now on,
Nike Striding Forward
always must be
"Nike of Samothrace."
We can never again say
just plain Nike, (was she ever plain?).
Now— fear of patent infringement—
we must specify terms
for all seven– and– one-half feet of her
wondrous coiled/uncoiled spring.
Here's a real two-thousand-year Swoosh.
Right foot firmly planted,
knee slightly bent, left toes
touching barely Ionian soil
as she lifts for the next step
through ages.
Nike
Striding Forward.

Put that in your sneaker.

enus de Milo –
A Farewell to Arms | *Fern G. Z. Carr*

with apologies to Ernest Hemingway

Venus de Milo, Alexandros of Antioch, circa 150 – 100 B.C.E.

Goddess of love and beauty,
saucy wench –
flaunting her perky breasts,
cloth drapery sliding
down her thighs
exposing
posterior cleavage
befitting a plumber.

She tilts to her right
unable to maintain balance,
still stumbling in a state of stupor
following an ambrosia
bender
culminating in the loss
of her cherished
plinth

and both marble arms.
She is now but
a spectacle
for Louvre tourists
who gawk and point
at the vestiges
of her night
of debauchery.

To Bellini | *F.J. Bergmann*

various sketches, Jacopo Bellini, 1424–1470

Jacopo, I am sorry that I couldn't afford the book
and only leafed through it in the back of the store.
Even at half price (one hundred twenty-five dollars before sales tax!)
it cost more than I've ever spent on literature or art at one go.
And, initially, I was disappointed:
your human figures are stodgy and sullen,
the drawing tentative, as if they didn't really hold your interest,
and the horses are disproportionately swollen,
with odd shapes and elongated limbs—
one could easily think that you had never seen a real one
and were drawing them as fabulous beasts,
approximating their appearance from familiar species.
The cheetahs, however, are not bad;
you drew them well, in elegant and playful poses,
and gave them pride of place in several major works
where the center of interest was really supposed to be
the petty nobleman or boozing mercenary commander
who had commissioned the piece.
And I also admire your lions,
rolling and biting and snoozing and fighting,
lifelike as if you had grown up in their company.
Perhaps the rarity of big cats from distant Africa
accounts for your careful attention to pelt and paw,
your skill in sketching tendon and skeleton.
But your dragons! Dragons embattled, wild and on the wing!
Intimate with the structure of each spurred membrane,
your sure hand materializes scale and vicious claw,
vivid as the scarred memory of war.
Dangerous and dazzling, terrible and true,
meticulous studies of the contorted anatomy of desire
rise in fire from smoky lines on old parchment.
Tell me, when you drew them, where were you?

the occult meaning of
the arnolfini wedding | *Steve Ely*

The Arnolfini Portrait, Jan Van Eyck, 1434

david eyck was right hernoult le fin
a shape shifting basilisk dripping
ducats and naranjas a yellow eyed
tongue flicking skin shedding skink
cloaked in sable darkness constanza
trenta virgin broodmare livebirthing
lizards from under her emerald
dagging into crowns and councils
and counting houses rothschilds
rockefellers saxe coburg gotha
hybrid bloodlines chimaeric dna
homo draconis the secret rulers of
the world they were taking no
chances cherry tree petit grifon saint
margaret of parturition annunaki
witchcraft from the lower fourth
dimension sounds crazy i know this
fucked up poetry with its liger aes-
thetic and tigon sensibility the writ-
ing sets you free the truth will make
you sick strap in enjoy the ride
stephanus ely fuit hic

Last Supper | *Doris Lueth Stengel*

The Last Supper, Leonardo Da Vinci, 1495 -1498

We arrive in Milano the day the exhibit reopens. Art experts had spent
21 years restoring the painting. Students, smug-full of knowledge, we
wait in herded groups inside thick cloister walls. Twentieth Century
technology electronically cleanses us of dust and pollutants. We walk
pure as apostles into the huge refectory where monks once ate in
silence, and some practical Father Superior ordered a door cut through
the end wall. Providing more direct access to the kitchen, even though
Christ's feet were cut off under the hanging tablecloth. Below those
wounded feet we stand, stunned by the size of the scene, smitten by
colors. Our guide points out the twelve grouped in trios around the
One centered in solitude. Their gesturing hands seem to ask, "Is it I,
Lord?" Each knows full well it could be he. Leonardo's presence
lingers near. These walls hold echoes of Napoleon's soldiers using
them for target practice, walls later leveled by Allied bombs.
A sandbag miracle saved the frescoed holy diners. We back away
fixated on the depth of Da Vinci's room and the meal that lasts
and lasts despite poor plaster and musket balls. Despite betrayal.

Mona Lisa Smiles | *Dan Fitzgerald*

Mona Lisa, Leonardo Da Vinci, 1503

Look at this poor sap
trying to become famous
by painting my picture.
I can see by the drawing
in the next room
that he already did my sister.
Wait till he finds out
I've given him the clap.

127

Mona Lisa and David | *Johnmichael Simon*

Mona Lisa, Leonardo Da Vinci, 1503 and David, Michelangelo, 1504

She was the match that lit the fire
that burns down the centuries
a darkish sweet mystery
her serene smile
so well known so loved
her thoughts her private existence
so little understood
where did she go after work?

And he
whose manly curves grace
a thousand books
was there a nice fire
glowing unseen in the background
to lull him into immobility?
Into which world did he step
after donning his robes
what kind of manuscripts did he enjoy
reading in the lonely evenings?

Had they lived on
as their effigies do
perhaps they may have met in the street
had a cup of coffee, a pizza, fallen in love
her match might have lit the coals of his fire
he might have bought her a ring
and she him a jock strap

Such are the flames of culture
that brighten the halls of the world
while we comfort ourselves anonymously
in their warmth
before going on our way

Lisa Gherardini
Might Be Pregnant | *Simon Peter Eggertsen*

Mona Lisa, Leonardo Da Vinci, 1503

Seated in a gray-clad museum wheelchair,
my father's brown eyes narrow, disappear as he ages,
    drifts toward a dream in the afternoon.
He ignores the art in the room, has not read the guide.
    His thoughts are elsewhere.
He imagines a touch, the soft embrace of a Venus
    with arms.
He wants to catch a ride across the gallery to meet her,
    again.

Across the room, Leonardo's *Mona Lisa* leans
    against her wall, out of reach of slashing fists.
Hands folded, soft *sfumato* eyes sleep weary,
    she smiles, bemused, down on him,
wonders why, unlike others, he is not paying
    attention to *her*.

Her middled age mocks him with veiled sweetness
and velvet, the moment's tease turns the edges of her
    thin-lipped mouth, barely.
Lower, in the silk folds of her black gown, she covers
    a soft secret.
She waits for him to guess it, or her true name, then she
will let him turn and go, even if to see another.
Strict as a Utah schoolmarm, she will give no hint to help him,
will hold her laconic smile until he makes his suggestive
    guess or just gives up and leaves.

Someone should tell him, "Lisa Gherardini might be pregnant."

Someone should tell her my father prefers Venus.

20

Tanka (statue of David) | *Tracy Davidson*

Statue of David, Michelangelo, 1504

statue of David
how visitors have admired
your chiseled features...
the years of smudged fingerprints
on your finely carved backside

Retrospect | *Peter Branson*

The Census at Bethlehem, Pieter Brueghel the Elder, 1566

In Breughel's masterpiece, Joseph and spouse
arrive at Bethlehem to pay their dues,
no hint, before celebrity kicks in,
they're more significant than other folk
out there, soused by the snow. This makes no sense
in geography nor when bowled over by
two thousand years' remorseless spin. Point is
it's what he liked to do – and understood.

Those who knew Newton as a problem child,
had they an inkling what he'd grow to do?
Could smug contemporaries at Eton sense
the Orwell rising in young Eric Blair?
All things are possible. In later years,
no doubt, drunk with hindsight, they drown in clues.

Frans Hals: Boy with a Lute
circa 1625 | *Gerald Locklin*

Frans Hals, Boy with a Lute, circa 1625

The kid is just a little ugly,
In the way the Dutch can be
When their crescent overbites
Push open their overly fleshy lips.
This one's hair's uncombed,
Unlike the perfect coiffures
Of all Hal's "Portrait(s) of a (Business) Man."
His hat's askew, as well. How effeminately,
Daintily, he tips his emptied glass to
Summon a refill, having probably
Spilled dregs on skeletal fingers and wrists.
He's even careless of his instrument. His
Type won't win many wars against Spain,
Except, perhaps, as little drummer boys.
Some folks pretend to admire this young
Lush's less commercial attitude towards
Life, but I know his type didn't last long
In the taverns I used to frequent. He'd
Better save his tips if he hopes ever to
Get laid much, or else become
A whore himself. And learn to shut
His homely mug before he gets
A Van Dick stuck in it.

Frans Hals: Portrait of a Woman, 1635 | *Gerald Locklin*

Frans Hals, Portrait of a Woman, 1635

This woman is identified as fifty-six
But looks ten or twenty years older,
And to dress in such silks, she must
Have had servants up the wazzoo.
She's also clutching a Bible,
Which means she's probably not getting laid—
No wedding ring either. Whereas I would
Have gladly bedded many comely
Fifty-six-year-old swimmers at the YMCA
Pool, even when I was a lot closer to their
Age. Women really are taking great care
Of their appearances these days, at least in
California, and probably Arizona too.
Well, they did have the consolations of
Religion back then, and a restorative
Afterlife, whereas most of the cults
Out here are kooky and suicidal: in place
Of the Body and Blood of Christ, they
Wash down arsenic with Kool Aid.
Or freeze to death on a mountain top,
Waiting in vain for the Spaceship Shuttle
To Rapture-Ville. This one could probably
Make a good nurse, though: change one's
Sheets and rub one's back. Now that I look
At her in that light, she's starting to seem a
Lot prettier. I bet they'd heard of
The Happy Ending Massage by then. They
Probably brought it back from Bangkok,
Like the Italians brought back spaghetti.

Guardroom with the Deliverance of Saint Peter | Maryann Corbett

Guardroom with the Deliverance of Saint Peter, David Teniers, circa 1647

The point is that tomorrow they will be killed,
those soldiers gambling in the center foreground
while at the back, in a mist of pastels
to the right of the vanishing point, Peter
is sprung from prison by the angel.

You, viewer, are presumed to know this—
to be a burgher of Antwerp, in 1650 or so,
and all too familiar with the concept
of dying on account of religion.
Herod, the offstage villain,
finding Peter gone, will interrogate the soldiers
and order their execution.
A verse of Acts will detonate
like a bomb at the roadside.

A hard sentence. Most artists play it down.
Their soldiers sleep, look drunk, sprawl over stairs,
low and off-center, out of the focal point,
arms flung across their faces, guilty. Footnotes.
Not Teniers. Notice what love he shows them—
these soldiers dragged into someone else's struggle—
by painting not the world of *anno Domini* 44
but the world he knows how to paint,
the dailiness of the Northern Baroque:

That coxcomb, front and center, with his curls,
his fashionable broad sash, his pink hose-points,
his eyes locked on the dice,
who will lose his money tonight and his life tomorrow—
see with what care Teniers has rendered the folds
of the soft, thin leather of his boots.
In the patina of cuirasses and gorgets,

see what pains he takes with the light of the world.

He has given his gifts entirely to them,
knowing they too will give everything,
Holy Innocents of a different kind,
collateral damage of the blast
of glory.

Working Late | *Phil Howard*

Officer and Laughing Girl, Johannes Vermeer, circa 1650s

When we talked that late Thursday afternoon
In the room where the documents were stored
For safekeeping during the evening and night,
Your face was illuminated by light
From the high window, it was early June.
That day I had been terminally bored

But, at that moment, I recalled the Vermeer,
The soldier and the laughing girl one
With the map of Holland on the back wall;
And, in that room in the dingy town hall,
I thought 'it's happening right now, right here',
And I returned your smile, composure gone.

Ode to Velázquez | *Alan Britt*

For José Rodeiro

Las Meninas, Diego Velázquez, 1656

A painter posing before the beveled mirror
of a bustling palace
has the dark look of curious confidence.

Nearby
women flow
across the parquet palace floor.

All the velvet alone that day
must've been worth thousands,
perhaps millions by today's standard.

Velasquez brushes plum blossoms
from the sultry lap
of daily royal existence.

He faces the mirror,
then steps through 500 years to smell
Cuban coffee brewing in José's kitchen.

Vermeer | *Wislawa Szymborska*

translated from the Polish by
Stanislaw Baranczak and Clare Cavanagh

The Milkmaid, Johannes Vermeer, circa 1658

So long as that woman from the Rijksmuseum
in painted quiet and concentration
keeps pouring milk day after day
from the pitcher to the bowl
the World hasn't earned
the world's end.

I Got Yer "Grumpy"
Right Here, Pal. | *Ron. Lavalette*

Snow White and the Seven Dwarfs; Folk tale collected by Grimm Brothers, 1812

I guess you'd be pretty grumpy, too
if you shared a crackerbox cottage
with six other chirpy little bastards,
up every day at the crack of dawn
with a merry *Hi-Ho, Hi-Ho* on their
lips, off to work after nothing but
a meager bowl of gruel, carrying
pickaxes and a box of dynamite,
leaving behind such a rare beauty,
a fair-skinned brown-eyed princess
to sweep up after them, make up
their beds, wash out their nasty
sheets, no one keeping her company
but a bunch of dopey bluebirds.
What a waste.
                And speaking of
dopey, let me just say a few words
about a couple of the schmucks
I work with:
                I busted a thumb
about a month ago and found out
Doc's not much of a real doc; and
I don't know what it is that keeps
that nitwit Sleepy nodding all day
or Happy so friggin happy, but
sooner or later there's bound to be
a cave-in and, frankly, I'll be glad
for the time off.
                Maybe then I'd
get to hang around the house,
see if the princess comes across
with a little TLC. Now, *that* might
improve my attitude some, eh?

Go away now, you're buggin me.

Frankenstein Birthdays | *Dan Fitzgerald*

Frankenstein, Mary Shelley - 1818, Boris Karloff - 1931, Peter Boyle - 1974

Today it is my hands,
tomorrow the feet.
Sometime next week,
the eyes have it.
Last month the liver turned two.
Ides of March the heart beat first,
missing its first valentine.
Tenth of May, the head celebrates.
Kidney, spleen, torso and all the rest,
don't seem to remember.
If there is any one day
to make it all seem real,
it would be the day
the brain first turned on.
That is the birthday I would
like to forget.

A Memory of Madrid | *Letitia Minnick*

Saturn Devouring His Children, Francisco Goya, circa 1820

I think I was fourteen on that summer trip to Spain.
Six students and a Spanish teacher
taking in the Museo del Prado
and the fine art of Castilian culture.
Feeling well equipped,
having fingered through my father's art books,
I passed each piece with appreciation
and more than a vague recollection.
It was only as I stopped to rest and raised my eyes
to the oil mural transferred to canvas
hanging directly across from me
that I was transfixed
staring into Saturn's bulging eyes.
It was if I had interrupted him mid-bite—
his gaping mouth about to close
on what remained of his son's left arm.
The small dark photo
on the clean white page of a coffee table tome
did not prepare me for the gore of Saturn
sinking his fingers
into the back of the headless bloody corpse—
a monstrosity almost five feet tall
and nearly a yard across.
One of Francisco Goya's "Black Paintings", I recalled
it had once adorned his dining room.
As I sat stunned, the thought came to mind that
Goya was crazy
and I should have studied French.

Mt. Fuji | *Kath Abela Wilson*

Mt. Fuji in Clear Weather, Katsushika Hokusai, circa 1830

7 clear summer evening
5 getting ready for
3 the great ball
3 Mt. Fuji
5 puts on her red dress

the diving bird | *Jim Bennett*

The Wreck Buoy, Joseph Mallord William Turner, 1849

the artist must have seen the bird
in its wild dive towards the sea

he painted the sweep of wing
the torpedo body

as it aims for water   a suggestion
caught in a smudge of paint

a moment's thought for colour
to sit against the dark grey sky

a flick of wrist
a blur at the edge of vision

look at that diving bird I said
what bird she asked

she did not see it   no one did
but it is there suspended forever

a streak of grey light
moments from its strike

On the Weeping Statue of Madonna | *Benjamin Taylor Lally*

The statue of the Virgin Mary at the Church of the Sacred Heart, Platina, Brazil,
Artist unknown, circa 1850

With furious passion, the newsmen invaded
the once-vibrant village to plunder for proof
that these visceral droplets were somehow related
to the uncanny absence of sickness. Find truth,
take a photograph, strike up some witnesses.
The newspaper editors, giggling, giddy,
scoff at the evidence, call it ridiculous,
and make it a front-page story. The city
never retreats from conveniently heart-
warming stories, but few will admit they believe
that such tales can be true in this era of science.
But the villagers noticed, before they'd depart,
the reporters and crews were reluctant to leave,
and would stare at the statue in almighty silence.

Advertising Arsenic | M.A. *Griffiths*

Madame Bovary, Gustave Flaubert, 1856

The image that sticks with me is Emma stuffing
whiteness into her mouth like sherbet powder.
She does it on the run, I think, her long skirts curling
around her legs like neglected cats. She swipes
her mouth with the back of her hand. Then she says,
half to herself, half to me: *I will lie down now*
and go to sleep. That's how we both want it:
the soft blink into a deep gentle end—but I know,
and how does she not know?—that there is pain
and retching, long hours stretched with suffering
till the body exhausts the light.
                                    Listen, Emma,
Woody Allen says he's not afraid of dying,
just doesn't want to be around when it happens.
We understand that, don't we? I understand you,
feel your desperation, the last leap into darkness
that turns out to be a flame. I would take your hand,
help you step over the stile of flesh into the green
and freedom of the next field, where they are picnicking
in a blur of meadow flowers. Instead we stick
here like flies nailed to a windscreen by a rush
of wind that chills our eyes.
                                    I will leave, Emma,
be gone finally, but you will always run and try
to escape. Your stomach will heave, your guts
will grind again and again, but you never lived.
You have that mercy, yet I cannot forget you,
cannot dislodge the teasel of you from my hair.
I carry your weight like an unwanted child.

The Wood | *Ackroyd Jackson*

Dante perdido na floresta, Gustave Doré, 1857

Nel mezzo del cammin di nostra vita
mi ritrovai per una selva oscura.

- Dante Alighieri, Inferno, Canto 1

i.

The dog is barking at the light,
it has become a catastrophe of teeth
yelping at a yellow bush, its six necks
entangled. It is hungry for more sun.

I run on into twig-shadow, until the slink
and sidle of the leopard sorts the trees,
and its neck elongates to a naked girl,
inscribing frankness in the frozen mud.

This is a pause on a stump of oak.
The air is a hand pressing down, turning our heads
to a dazed brook full of dead toads.
In the ditch bracken rusts, limp with winter.

A fish bursts up out of the ice,
twirling with self-satisfaction, its colours
preen in the day: *all the rivers are mirrors*
we laugh, and stare into them, enraptured.

You are standing at the crossroads
announcing that you would prefer to have taken
the path I have taken, that life lacks justice,
and benevolence is useless in this wood.

I grow angry, and throw my fists at my thighs,
and boot a dead tree. I decide to broadcast
the murder I am in love with, whose detail

surprises you by its meticulousness.

You say that now you will spend the remainder of life
plotting to make sure I don't enjoy this wood.
You say you will torch the heather, and already
imagine a scar of burning, and me alone in it.

ii.

Happiness is possible, you intone,
in another part of the wood, in a column of sun.
You are increased strength: your life is heavy,
but you are starting to accept this wood.

The blackberry is shrivelled and green like a pea,
but it will be fruit for bird and man.
Dullness of the body is a hidden good:
our failings always transfer us towards absolutes.

You must never ignore the shape of duty,
you yawn, as these birds can't, or else they'll die:
whatever your reason for procrastination,
waiting will cede worse. Stay busy.

I find that I now love this wood,
the leopard is saying, curling up in the centre of the path.
His verdict doesn't elevate his estimation
of himself, he only smiles and falls asleep.

I rise, and seek out the best section of river,
your favourite spot, and discover an inscription
in underlined characters, written with a twig.
The earth reads: 'I'm happy that you're sitting here'.

Not everything is perfect in the wood,
the aquifers are low with the sin of the world,
and our signature additions to the crisis
are contemptible, but I'm calm about our faults.

We are against the proliferation of this disaster.

One way to be happy in the wood
is to forgive it, and love it liberally.
As you sleep you seem to be growing in size.

iii.

The otter is lapping at the water, restored
to health in winter, nurtured throughout spring,
and given his right capacity for life by summer.
His happiness is a gift proffered to the wood.

We were entwined today under the apple tree,
your softness was the impossibility of others,
your flesh created instances of good everywhere.
The leopard also announced it had fallen in love.

All day the sun is in constant deliberation
and we follow it over the stiled bridge,
through the corridor of birch onto the ranges.
The heather beyond is shining with gossamer,

and the completeness of our acceptance of this wood
is a permanent accompaniment to our walking.
And so we walk, having forgotten death,
rejecting nothing, finding hope restored in all things.

Our interests have been united by a question
and its perfect answer. 'I' and 'you'
have become 'us'; like this, we go scenting
the ragwort, and picking the plump blackberries.

The dog is docile, padding up to us under the ash,
he licks our hands and feet contentedly.
Nothing is wrong here, or could be wrong,
the world's apotheosis is reconcilement to itself.

We lack the contentious motion, the dutiful war,
but we aren't bereft of purpose, there is too much here:
strawberry and bracken, deer and spider.
At night we breathe in unison with the wood.

Peasant Bathing | *Perie Longo*

The Goose Girl, Jean Francois Millet, 1863

My mother always said she married
my "common stock" father
to balance her southern "aristocracy."
A Daddy's Girl, no wonder I'm drawn
to the Goose Girl, her clothes flung off
in forest shadows where the cow grazes
and the artist works breathless, brush
trembling, a gaggle of geese nearby.
Thinking herself alone, a little warm,
she tests the brook's coolness with her toe.
I'm reminded of a time hiking on a hot
summer day, I came upon a river,
its ripples struck with irresistible light.
I told my husband to stand guard
should some stray happen along
and stripped right there in the woods,
plunged in among ducks and dragonflies,
relieved in the bliss of my bathing.
Then the call, "people coming."
Around the bend came a whole gaggle
of boy scouts. We gawked at each other,
me half in, half out blushing, their mouths
hanging open at my ample breasts,
my husband brushing them off.

What My Autistic Son Might Say to Vilhelm Hammershoi | *April Salzano*

Vilhelm Hammershoi, 1864-1916

Thank you for the dying light,
the dancing dust motes,
the rooms that are anything
but empty. Places are always fullest
when they seem to be deserted. Panes
form perfect angles, contrasted by light.
A singular figure only
appears to be remaining,
intentionally positioned facing away,
only as important as a piece of furniture,
a complimenting vertical placement
to restore balance.
I too see exactly and only
what is there, the beauty
of what is not.

After the Last Spaceship | *Deborah P. Kolodji*

The Ragpicker, Edouard Manet, 1865

Twenty rotations
of this dusty planet—
no one's coming back
to this barren place.

A fixture on the corner
of an abandoned spaceport,
he has a hole in the left knee
of weatherproof pants.

Manet's ragpicker
embodied in shadowed eyes,
a walking stick in hand,
trash by his foot.

His overgrown beard
hides life sorrows
in the way of vagabonds
from inhabited spheres.

A dying world's value
borne in a shoulder sack
with no one else available
to shoulder the load.

After Auguste Renoir's "Lunch at the Restaurant Fournaise" | *Cynthia Gallaher*

Lunch at the Restaurant Fournaise, August Renoir, 1875

They tricked her for awhile,
and now she must decide
between them.

There was that foggy night she strolled
with Alain along the Seine smoking
hand-rolled cigarettes,

Then the light-dappled morning Albert took her
by hand to La Rive Gauche
to see plein air artists at work.

Each claimed to be Auguste,
assuming the middle name of their creator
and the fiery month their love began.

It is now June 31st,
and again by river, together,
miles from Paris,

The brothers rent a skiff for an hour
then treat her to midday wine
and respite at Fournaise.

Amid their latticed truths,
they lean back for her answer.
Albert stares with admiration.

Alain feigns coolness
while delft blue flowers
belie his smoldering passion.

Her hand grazes her mouth.
She speaks.
"The two of you will do just fine."

Isle of the Dead | *Daniel Y. Harris*

Isle of the Dead, Arnold Böcklin, 1880

Steals the corpse and faces the watergate
with its sharp islet and steers a gaunt, white
figure, maneuvering its rowboat from the

stern. The oarsman's yellow, fetid hair
drooped over his red ears, hears the faint,
whisked laughter of waves resist brown

oars. Cypress trees hemmed in by ports,
engrave the rocks, are molested, cold,
blue-black by salty, sea air with the gray

hum of stench rot rising with bony gulls—
soils canvas with mustard chiascuro, and
now, emptied of color, sees itself on the

green hill with the crescents of wolf eyes.

The Door Effect | *Brooke Dorn*

unknown artist

The painting I found at a local thrift shop quickly became a bore.
Even with all of it's beautiful colors, the painting was still of a door.

Squinting in the Light | *Brooke Dorn*

Starry Night, Vincent Van Gogh, 1889

The blue and yellow swirls make the night sky come alive.
The moon resembles the sun.
The stars are not stellar, but exist in compliance.
While reality comes undone.
I squint my eyes at it's beauty and wish that
        my computer screen was bigger.

A Laundromat | *Douglas Richardson*

Starry Night, Vincent Van Gogh, 1889

a laundromat
in the starry night
just you and a woman
who looks familiar
she hums a melody
that travels
like myth
down your spine
your clothes spinning
safe and warm
in the machines

The Bite | *Dušan Čolović*

Wheat Field with Cypresses, Vincent van Gogh, 1889

Gilded wheat spike
of a disquiet quake
I inhale the nectar of the moment
a breeze washes my dreams
in the soul's membrane
a flame reflects
under the sun's eyebrow
in a charmed meadow
through a quiver
a new summer is resurrected.
Imprinted
upon a slice of bread
is the God's Bite.

Van Gogh Self-Portrait | *Helen Bar-Lev*

Self Portrait, Vincent Van Gogh, 1889

Brush strokes swirl his face
stir the air around him
into a halo of colours
blue eyes agonized
by their own brilliance

An Apple | *Martin W. Bennett*

Still Life with Apples, Paul Cézanne, 1890

Provenance a mystery, down the carriage aisle
rolls this apple, rolls and veers and rolls up
to the sliding doors, wobbles before it settles,
a pale green, somewhat improbable fullstop –

overworld and underworld come together
with a doff of the hat at Magritte.
Today being Saturday and no commuter on the seat
opposite, distant schoolboy memories of 'Finders, keepers;

losers, weepers': Something for nothing, early morning windfall!
Besides, who ever declined a free breakfast, above all
during these lean times when each month's end stalks
like an accountant with potentially ruinous powers –

Prompting the 64 cent question, to pocket or not to pocket it?
Peckishness knows only one answer, the quicker the better,
without risk of getting caught. Except, fruit once snatched,
I find myself assailed by misgivings as old as Adam,

as though this small sub-suburban instance contained
a re-enactment of the Fall: Guilt or mental itch? Then,
glimpsed a few seats down, the bag whence the apple came;
smile of the owner while I walk over, hand it back –

Mind's eye switching to those depicted by Paul Cezanne,
'so radiantly serious, so true'; Cox, Pippin or Granny Smith,
the one which dropped on Newton's head, logo of Gravity –
What, here on earth and beyond, keeps everything in place.

Monet In Harmony | *Mary Harwell Sayler*

Cathedrale de Rouen, Plein Soleil, Claude Monet, 1892

Not the light but
impressions of the light –
not the cathedral but
colors dissolving like
wafers on the tongue.

Someday you'll go
and see what drew him:
the golden tones, the
content wavering.

First Impression Epigrams | *Neal Whitman*

Children at Play on the Beach, Edward Henry Potthast, 1896

Until you can swim
go in only belly-button-deep.
Does the "30-minutes after-you-eat" rule
still apply?

Studies show that children
laugh 400 times a day.
Adults only fourteen.
Is that why children live longer?

Dogs on the beach
are so happy to see each other.
Why do I detest
people at the airport?

Rodin Speaks with his Hands | *Jerry Quickley*

For C.C.

The Thinker, August Rodin, 1902

The Thinker
has hands and feet that are just a little too large for
his body

over and over again in Rodin's work
Bodies perfectly proportioned
all except the hands and feet
too large
slightly distorted

The artist's clear metaphor

subject's hands and feet
gnarled and scarred from the
weight of existence   layered betrayals
They'd walked great distances
carried heavy burdens
they existed
and Rodin knew that
they'd need big hands and feet

the ones we were given are too puny
for the tasks of this world
tiny castors on immense bodies of work
requiring dainty waltzes through valleys
where blind spirits push whimsy and boulders
where great bodies of memory are authored
through equal parts fear and glacier

We walk in places where backs are broken
as easily as promises
Rodin travels with me
and shows me what's needed to survive

the span of his art evokes twinklings
as precious and transient as a child's yawn
holding me up like a suspension bridge
gazing at the water and rocks
roaring below

He had passed on by the time I was born
He had passed on by the time I was grown
He had passed on by the time my hands
grew large enough to sustain memories
and hold children
He had passed on by the time my feet
broadened to size 17
and helped distance me from the sweep of chaos
and the derisive primacy of my most distant glaciers
that still blot the sun and play host to
my antiquities
my ellipses
my confirmations and retributions
grace and slur all in the same breath
firm beliefs in gardens that don't bloom and play host
to absenteeism and crooked choices

congregations of pack animals
bipedal promises and knuckle-walking
cuneiform details that fix results
and insure liberty is as likely
as hugging the sun
The fix is in
and the closest you get to love
is to bask in it's promise
as you keep close to the pack
just in case you're wrong
just in case your feet aren't big enough
just in case your hands aren't strong enough
just in case the flash blinds you
and Rodin can no longer help

Before The Canvas | *Timothy Charles Anderson*

A Bold Bluff, C.M. Coolidge, circa 1903

Was there anyone bothered
that the artist brought the easel
and the brushes to the parlour

Because he could have been
signaling somebody, from that angle
most cards were in easy view

Coolidge clearly was an artist
of integrity, silent, as chips slid
back and forth, bets raised

Sweat glistened on the judge's nose
—a tell—still no one knew
until the bogus hand had landed

Therefore we surmise
he was an honest man, faithfully
representing the game of poker

I guess he didn't embellish
—add extra chips to the stack
or make two pair into a flush

Maybe he won them over
with a joke, drawing them
another drink or lighting their cigars

Good guy to have around
when the barking starts and nobody
is allowed to leave the table

Do Not Cast Your Runes
Mr. James | *Alan Price*

Casting the Runes, M.R.James, 1911

It wasn't the boy, in the park, chased by the hopping white creature.
It wasn't the insects, climbing out of the scary magic lantern slide.
It wasn't the alchemist, Karswell, reading odd books
    at the British museum.
It wasn't the slip of paper, passed on to Harrington, and the demon.

But it was, when Dunning found a mouth, with teeth, under his pillow.

It was the fact that I, like Dunning, also kept my watch there.
It was the fact that, aged thirteen, I was afraid of the bed sheets.
It was the fact that, heart beating, I hid under the freezing duvet.
It was the fact that I never knew who actually turned of the light.

The Poet at 3 O'clock | *Bruce Taylor*

The Poet at 3 O'clock, Mark Chagall, 1912

If the soldier in the snow's
that happy of course
his hat would float above
his upside down head,
If a giant rooster played
a violin, it would be a blue one.

If the lovers at their windy promenade
were not aware of this apparition why
would they fly each other like kites?

p25 (handwritten)

Nude Descending a Staircase | *Alan Wickes*

For Mike Alexander

Nude Descending a Staircase, Marcel Duchamp, 1912

The obvious question no one ever asks *a*
is why descend a staircase in the nude? *b*
Giorgione's Sleeping Venus calmly basks *a*
within a green Arcadian dream imbued *b*
with golden light, while Sandro's Aphrodite *c*
drifts shore-wards in a coy pubescent pose *d*
A classicist myself, I shun the sprightly *c*
preferring nudes depicted in repose; *d*
although an antelope in flight looks sleek *e*
not so the human. In truth, athletic *f*
heroes 'a la Greque' who proudly streak *e*
towards the winning post, seem unaesthetic *f*
We note a slight anatomical failure:
God-like physique, but boyish genitalia. *near rhyme* (handwritten)

58

136

Quiet city | *Mantz Yorke*

Melancholy and Mystery of a Street, Giorgio de Chirico, 1914

We look back: golden concrete,
phalanxed in black, shrinks
into the distance. The litter of boxes,

cans and plastic bags we left
has been efficiently cleaned up:
only the darkness of buildings remains
twisted in the gutter. No one moves

outside their black-glazed blocks
at this hour – the shadow stretching towards us
from a side-street might be a statue

for all we know. Columns
are scratching at the foundations'
decaying cement, and ivory shoots
are searching beneath the slabs

for cracks of light. Thinly,
keener than a muezzin's call,
a solo trumpet slices through the calm.

If Jeffrey Smart Painted
James Joyce | Desmond Kon

Portrait of the Artist, James Joyce, 1916

*I must have looked like a fellow throwing a handful of peas into the air.
People began to look at us. She shook hands a moment after
and, in going away, said she hoped I would do what I said.*

- James Joyce

It would have been in Rathgar, outside a steel mill.

The building seated in its shadow, top row of windows
now shattered glass – a boy facing east, hurling balls of coal.
There was an ice climber's cord hanging from his outpost,
knotted with caster wheels. It looked like a rope ladder.

Smart used a disegno, measured every angle, each inch
of scaffolding another space for a softer bit of street yellow.

The brick orange was added for Joyce's cheekbones.

I saw Keats returning from the rose garden with a sonnet.
The garden belonged to an old miner, its bushes brittle and dry.
It looked strange, a small cottage surrounded by a picket fence,
and beside it, a landfill that ran a mile into Naul Hills.

Yet free of it. Keats had fallen asleep, the way Severn sketched him.
Fanny Brawne in relief, standing a few yards from him.
Near another window, a barn swallow eating from her hand.

The painting looked like a pastoral. Idyllic. Distant.
Crepe roses behind Joyce. Stadium lights. The freeway of no cars.

Living in the city is deafening. London teaches you
to ignore the immediate moment, the overturned crate in the alley.
Bags of beans split open. Sprawling lentils. Lima beans, pinto beans.

Your eyes turn lazy, the stoplight to tell you when to stall or go.

The bin to throw your brown bag into. London forcing you
to locate particularity – things, relevance, connection, longing as love.
Something to be done. The route to the library where you'll sit
in the far right corner, on the big chair riveted to the ground.

It was closing time at the mill, black mask of figures in contrapposto.

The disegno looked like an origami pattern for a rose,
its mosaic tiling of mountain folds, ridge folds and valley folds.

The boy took it in his hand, placed the coal neatly within it.
Wrapping it in, he handed it to Smart and asked for a drawing.

The warmth of sepia light | *Sonja Smolec*

Seated Nude, Ca., Amedeo Modigliani, 1917

Sometimes, in dreams, I find myself
shaped like Modigliani's lewd portraits
of nude women who, with no sense of sin, offer
their fine, sunny colored
rounded thighs and breasts.

*

My dreams never fade,
I will never leave them
like some people do with old paintings
dumped in a far, dark corner
because they can't see
how precious they are,
and they value them mostly
by the frame.

*

In the morning I will lean my head
on my left shoulder to avoid the light
coming between the curtains,
maybe I will forget to cover
my yawning mouth and you will see
my back teeth's white fillings
before I call your name.

*

Come, breathe with me the scent
and the warmth of a new morning's
sepia light.
Put your palm on my chest,
paint me with the rest of the spilled colors
and feel how the sun rises again.

In Chrustov's House
Near St. Prex | *Kenneth Pobo*

In Chrustov's House Near St. Prex, Marianne von Werefkin, circa 1917

A single blossom sets a table
cloth on fire. When you sit alone
behind a plate, your life over
or seeming that way, the bouquet

says that the river inside the heart
that can't be crossed stills
and allows passage. Dishes negotiate
the tiny space between us,

less than an inch apart,
with a floury smell. The lamp
that tenuously hangs knows your name
and secrets. Night thickens like batter.

In the morning you spread butter on,
forget all the arguments you had
about truths that suddenly seem like snow
easing down a pane.

131

Golden Boy | *Fern G. Z. Carr*

Golden Boy, Georges Gardet, 1918

Bronze Adonis gilt in gold
balanced atop the dome
of the Legislative Building,
cradling a sheaf of wheat
and raising a torch

like a relay runner
poised to pass the baton;
you are toned, buff –
in the buff.

Naughty naked boy,
where is your
common sense –
facing northward
flaunting your manhood
and exposing your full
glory
to raw Winnipeg winters?

The Bath | *Ellaraine Lockie*

The Bath, Paul Klee, 1919

She stares straight ahead
Stretched out soaking au naturel
in a stark white tub
and trance-like state
Blind to his brush strokes
Pierre Bonnard's wife subject
Portrayed at a time
when water therapy
was treatment for tuberculosis
Or obsessive neurosis
One wonders whether she
wasn't already dead
The water having fatally failed
And the corpse prepared for viewing
with oil paint preservation
Bonnard's depiction
a conjugal composition inquest
Or whether she has
succumbed to coma
Paint-paralyzed by the parade
of people invading her privacy
The Tate Gallery
a modern municipal bathroom

Wonder-worker | *Michael Virga*

The day after Christmas, Norman Rockwell, 1922

Santa's sack emptied
now he's sacked out:

spent on childhood

Magritte's *Lovers* | *Eric Evans*

The Lovers, Renée Magritte, 1928

They kiss a kiss only lovers can,
their mouths darkened by shadow,
his knowledge of her clockwise
swirl, her proclivity to trace
his lips. But, limited as we are,
we only assume they kiss between
those covers. They may be trading
secrets or carrying on an ancient
fight, telling tales or passing
a key to unshackle limbs from
an unseen chair. They are lovers,
or so we're led to believe – we
don't know what they do, only what
we think we'd do in their place.

Untitled by Paul Klee | *Ellaraine Lockie*

untitled, Paul Klee, circa 1930

You have so eloquently
labeled your art
And I so ineptly
escape your logic
The Donkey where
I see a pig
Pickle the Clown
who looks to me
like a native Indian dancer
Juggles in April
a map mangled in midair
Although I do see
California community manners
in your *Neighborhood Doors* maze
I can't for the life of me
find a female form
in the folds of *Hero Mother*
Yet I come to an inked pond
floating on gold-edged paper
with graphic birds
trees and wetland grass
And you've tagged it *Untitled*

I Am Rhinoceros | *A.J. Huffman*

The Persistence of Memory, Salvador Dali, 1931 and
Rhinoceros Dressed in Lace, Salvador Dali, 1956

in lace dress, shredded, blowing
(it was a bitch to get it
over my horns). In desperately dull
desert winds, I wander and wonder
What is the point? This menial existence
rains existential chaos, holds no cosmic
meaning, only occasional comedic value.
Droll backroom chitters, the fire that fuels
me, I thrust forward, onward
over / under / through ever-
elongating hands
                            dripping time,
an interesting shade of disharmony, to paint
my toes.

The Bride | *Salvatore Difalco*

The Bride of Frankenstein, Directed by James Whale, 1935

In a subplot of the novel, she was the consort
Created for the Monster, but never brought to life.
In the Hollywood adaption of the story,
She hissed like a swan in a wedding dress

And bandages leftover from *The Mummy*.
The buzzy Neferetiti coif and lightning streaks
Immortalized her as a horror queen
And go-to shtick for Halloween.

Real life child of radical Bohemians
And true wife to the Hunchback of Notre Dame,
She ran a London dance school
In the Isadora Duncan style,

And also sang: "Songs for a Shuttered Parlour,"
"Songs for a Smoke-Filled Room."
The song about her husband's
"Clock" not working for her.

Good old Boris, burned and scarred, offered
Subtle shadings of emotion, as one might
Surviving mill-fire flames, and infamy.
His vocabulary bloomed to fifty words.

Clive was trashed, but Whale did not recast his gig
As Pretorius, needing not only his florid hysterics
But also the whisper of camp he and Thesiger
Breathed into the film.

The harrowing homunculi were tiny, driven actors
Stuffed in giant jars against black velvet,
Rotoscoped and matted into the narrative:
Little cogs and wheels of the horror's motor.

The shot of Boris loping through a graveyard
To a figure of the crucified Christ was nixed
By censors, so as not to traumatize the audience
Or galvanize the Satanists among them.

In the end nothing is resolved except destruction.
The bride rejects the Monster like a banshee.
The laboratory crackles; the castle falls.
Off in the wings, the Hunchback applauds.THE FRIGHTENERS

Landscape from a Dream | *Catherine Graham*

Landscape from a Dream, Paul Nash, circa 1936

Two skies in this mind game:
one sunlit   the other blood-stained.

A large mirror and empty frames?
Strange
how the spheres bounce into the distance,
their shadows reversed.

The reddened sky terrifies me.
I'd swear   if I look closely

I see a kneeling rifleman
behind your menacing black bird.

The Firing Squad | *Johnmichael Simon*

Woman With a Hairnet, Pablo Picasso, 1938

They filed in blindfolded
stood akimbo to the wall
         the words

Blesseds dropped in the first salvo
then kings, altars, promises,
sins, obedience,
disobedience stood for a while
bullets whistling by
then it dropped too

Most adjectives and adverbs
simply exploded of their own accord
as did many nouns of the higher sphere
abstractions, inventions, musings,
articles, conjunctions
and the like

When the smoke cleared
and the stage was swept
only the most stalwart
nouns and verbs
were left standing

'Let's write an epitaph for them'
said eyes to hat
lips smiled
'let's paint a picture'
'something abstract and meaningful
like a Picasso'
suggested nose
and was shot immediately

After their blindfolds were removed
the rest of them sat down
with crayons and finger paint
and started to work

Reflection | *Kathleen M. Krueger*

Mother and children on the road, Dorthea Lange, 1939

you live by default

no decision brought
you here

don't think, don't question
do what needs to be done

at the moment
to survive

it's easier that way

feed the children
fuel the car

sleep
drive
sleep

I recognize you
I've seen you

in the mirror

Why Policemen Stopped Flying | *Paula McKay*

13⁄8

Death of Constable Scanlon, Sidney Nolan, 1946

Scientific studies confirm policemen once flew.
With thick plumage and a six foot wingspan
they used their legs as rudders to steer;
chests parallel to the sunburned earth.

Adapted to the Southern hemisphere
they laid their eggs one or two at a time
in small dark cells for security
next to batons and shiny whistles.

Eating what they wanted, mostly fast food
hot dogs on the wing, they flew in a flock
in a northerly or easterly direction
beating air in a felony of feathers
like Lucy in the sky with handcuffs
their cry almost human.

Evidence suggests policemen surrendered flight
during the Cellium Vulgaris age
a period when Celtic iron-clad humans
took to shooting *coppers* with a gun.

Cellium Vulgaris, commonly called
Ned Kelly, with metal carapace and mask
forced policemen out of trees to plod the earth
to hunt and kill on equal terms.

Thus: one more amazing creature now extinct.

Poem inspired by Andrew Wyeth's The Revenant | *Marie Lecrivain*

The Revenant, Andrew Wyeth, 1949

In between waiting for tasks
to finish & wishing for
affections to end,
you find yourself
filled with light
& unraveling
around the edges,
slightly confused
as well as repulsed
by your artistry.

The truth; you are
an accidental alchemist,
peripherally aware
of the magic
you have wrought
without, as well as
within.

You

A...

R...

E...

... a...w... a... k... e...

& try not to forget,
before you fall
into the shadows
of sleep & care,
before you
veil your brow
& mistake
this moment
a dream...

the beautiful | *Kevin Cornwall*

Blue in Green, Miles Davis, 1959
Bindweed - dodder, Chi Bai Shi, 1954 and
An Ordinary Evening in New Haven, Wallace Stevens, 1950

L'exactitude n'est pas la verite.
- Henri Matisse

Caught up in the roof
there are leaves in the skylight
and, in the pool this morning,
clouds. Someone must decide.

There is a border of flowers
and a snarl of wild flowers
among them giving over to weeds
beneath the trees in half-leaf.

The decision whether to leave
or remove is moot
when working indelible colors in
retentive media: when

Miles Davis muffed a note
in the 8th measure of his solo
on "Blue in Green",
in 1959, he left it
just the way he played it;

in ninety years' Chi Bai Shi's
hsieh-i of bindweed,
a bamboo stalk wavers
where his hand trembled
over a moment of youthful folly;

and in Wallace Steven's heaven,
just as in New Haven,
no blossoms ever have
kept their bloom. Now,

there is something to decide,
a question to answer about
something important, something
gathering in the half-light.

Dali Rage | *Graham Fulton*

Christ of Saint John of the Cross, Salvador Dali, 1951

At the foot of *Christ of Saint John of the Cross*
a man in a Seventies Soviet top
with CCCP in big white type
gets miffed as he tries to photograph
the immaculate oil on his *Virgin* Phone.

Excuse me he tuts to pensioner gangs
who shuffle his arty field of fire.
Worshippers keep on barging across
with buggies, crisps and *Somerfield* bags.

He turns an atheist shade of red.
He feels as if he's about to burst.

A small boy with a Roman helmet
squeezes and weaves his way to the front,
determined to get a place
at the crucifixion, Jesus without a face,

hanging a mile above the sea.
Everyone loves a madman with taste.
Forgive them Sal, they know not what
they do. Messiahs bring out the worst.

The Day I Had the
Terrible Fear | *Laurel Ann Bogen*

The Day the Earth Stood Still, directed by Robert Wise, 1951

The Big No sits on my chest
and I think I'm only 56
but the invitation remains

Hi ya How ya doin?
have some coffee and some pie
have a serrated bread knife

I cannot name it yet
it squanders my daylight
black familiar coin
of the psycho trade
I remember it each time
it leaves me crouched
and flinching
still I brazen
fate and furies after a fashion
The Big No is indiscriminate
it doesn't care that I'm a Famous Los Angeles Poet
it will erode everything
it takes away the words, man
it takes away the words

To A Nameless French Woman Circa 1957 | *Eric Evans*

Bon Jour, Paris, Michel LeGrand, 1957

Oh, beautiful woman on the cover
of Michel LeGrand's *Bonjour Paris*,
where are your pants? And, for
that matter, who cares? The over-sized
shirt draped to mid-thigh is perfect
in its suggestion, its hemline hinting
just enough at the curves beneath.

I look at you with your arms thrown
open and doors flung wide, your
tousled hair and painted nails,
and I'm beyond sold, drawn to those
calves, tensed and tight, primed
to leap from the balcony and into
the sensuality of the Parisian day.

Take me with you, half-dressed
woman, take me with you, I want
to murmur into what I'm sure is
a perfumed neck, take me with
you as we seek food and wine and
the coolness of shadows within which
to properly introduce ourselves.

Tracks | *Donald Mulcahy*

Hound in Field, Alex Colville, 1958

the tracks in the snow
I dream of
belong to an albino wolf
curly as a sheep
with soft hazel eyes
with no look
of primal preoccupation
about them
and as I follow
the regularly spaced
five-toed paw prints
I come upon
open patches
of tawny winter grass
and all that is needed
to complete this picture
is a beagle
black, tan and white
running, turning
as a jack rabbit
piebald about the ears
leaps out from under a bush
and I know it's spring
and this is a painting
by Alex Colville
in which I don't belong

Still Life of an Artist | *Rosalee Thompson*

Coffee, Richard Diebenkorn, 1959

Black memory box
icicle tears
Mother says we need angel hair
My icicle tears freeze the tree

I can add but not subtract
I saw Superman cry once
I see a thousand buzzing red lights next to your one

Because of your unbearable beauty I will cut my hair
                                             I will cut my skin

So much can grow in this
one white gardenia
You can fuck me
but you can't watch me pray
Imagine a dove kissing your mouth

Oldenburg's Bride | *Eric Lawson*

Bride Mannikin, Claes Oldenburg, 1961

and soft scissor-shaped pillows
She liked the grips because they
creaked and the soft scissors
because they were useless
Just like her husband

She always wore green stockings
and blue and pink pantyhose
She insisted upon wearing these
items because they comforted her
and because they annoyed others
Just like her husband

She loitered every day at the
truck stop under the Pepsi sign
Cigarettes in a pack
Chocolates in a box
Pentecostal cross
All were on her person
All were her lucky charms
All reminded her of her carefree
and fun single life in the city
But that life is long gone now
Just like her husband

A Last Hurrah | *David Chorlton*

Tea Party, Philip C. Curtis, 1963

They're obviously from the age before ours;
two ladies at the table with hands
folded on their laps, a third
in evening dress with a matching scarf
caught in the breeze of time,
and a man the size of a child sitting on the porch's edge
not knowing where to look. The woodwork
is the immaculate achievement of someone
who cares, someone for whom
it was necessary to ornament as well as to contain
a space. Even surrounded
by hard earth and rock,
every detail from a pillar's base
to the fine strips cut by a loving knife
and the circular reliefs set just below the overhang
bears a craftsman's fingerprints.
Nothing is served to suggest
an imminent change, but this
is the last tea

before machines arrive
to strip the landscape to its veins of ore.

American Collectors | *Robert Wynne*

American Collectors, David Hockney, 1968

The Weismans inhabit their sculpture garden
like they've collected each other, late sun

throwing long shadows across the sparse scene.
Marcia's white teeth and pink caftan serve as beacons

next to a young tree in its pale terra cotta pot.
Fred is fixed firmly in place behind 3 rocks

stacked waist-high. He faces to the right
so he could be looking at his bright wife

or the very blue sky, or even the totem pole
peeking over some low shrubs and grinning

like the only one who's ever been in on the joke.

After Jim Nutt's
"Da Creepy Lady" | Cynthia Gallaher

Da Creepy Lady, Jim Nutt, 1970

Da Creepy Lady has linebacker shoulders.
Da Creepy Lady squeezes into asymmetrical pumps.
Da Creepy Lady walks a worldly tightrope
        held up by lipstick icicles.
Da Creepy Lady wants to climb the ladder of success
        but realizes it's all a shell game.

Da Creepy Lady's bra might fit
        Arnold Schwarzenegger
        if he became a she-man.
Da Creepy Lady's hairpiece
        could be early Egyptian
        but the late part of World War II interfered.

Da Creepy Lady's accidental pee
        takes a running leap
        and freezes mid-air.
Da Creepy Lady prefers following men
        with D.A. haircuts
        glistening as the coats of racehorses.

Da Creepy Lady doesn't know latitude from longitude
        but has entertained appendages of both persuasions.
Yet Da Creepy Lady's sapphire claws have wreaked havoc
        on many a masculine hide.

Da Creepy Lady is a name that
        even after decades you can't forget.
Da Creepy Lady's daddy is a Nutt case.

Da Creepy Lady towers above Chicago skyscrapers.
Da Creepy Lady's mustard-smeared view of the world
        has left her with ketchup on her face.

Da Creepy Lady tries to make an angry fist, but it's already in one.
Da Creepy Lady frames her world in leopard print
        to make her seem less the beast.

Da Creepy Lady consults high-priced genies
        and buys bargain table underwear that cause wedgies.
Da Creepy Lady chagrins and tries make it up to her boyfriend,
        but he feels as if his balls are six-feet under, and he's
        mad as hell.

Cows | *Simon Jackson*

Atom Heart Mother album cover, Hipgnosis, 1970

They know the end is coming.
They carry the knowledge of violent destruction
welling up within huge, sad eyes.
It is not despair that makes them move that way,
one slow joint slotting into the next,
each step slumped like a dropped sack of manure.
It is not despair, it is acceptance.
Buddhas of the grasslands,
the sideways chomp is a meditation,
the lowing moan an incantation,
the universal om channelled through soft throats
held low to the ground.
They guide in the apocalypse,
Low, pendulous udders counting down,
laden with milk that none will drink.

A Time Comes When You
No Longer Think It | *M.J. Iuppa*

Nude Elke 2, George Baselitz, 1976

1.

Slumped upside down in a straight back chair,
naked, feet pushed together– knees apart–
hands crossed at the wrist– folded
like sparrow wings, covering
a transparent nest.

2.

Hiding out in the open is the last place
anyone looks– smudge of charcoal
above your breast– bottleneck–
your face gone ashen, swallowing
your tongue.

3.

Colder still. The studio's chiaroscuro.
A curse or kiss could finish you.
His paint. His smell.
His clothes piled on the chair
behind you.

4.

How does it work to be elsewhere
when you're here?
The pose you hold indefinitely
crowds him. You can tell
by the way he steps back.

Dada Dada Boo Boo | *Mick Moss*

Dada exhibit at the Tate Modern, London, 1977

Dada came to London
in 1977
at the Tate
being a fan
I made a big effort
shiny red shoes
pink beret
and blue overalls
with WANKER
tastefully stencilled
across the back in
brilliant white emulsion
they didn't get the joke
and I was politely
asked to leave

After Roger Brown's "The Leaning Tower of Touhy" | *Cynthia Gallaher*

The Leaning Tower of Touhy, Roger Brown, 1980

Take one: The Leaning Tower of Pisa
Take two: The Leaning Tower of Touhy
Take three: Roger Brown's painting of The Leaning Tower of
Touhy.

From its pinnacle, a 1940s pouf-haired,
shirt-waisted gal poses and waves.
It's a Chi-town photo op
a mere mile from SuperDawg drive-in.

Half the height and tilt of the Italian original,
you'd never guess it from the snapshots,
or those gasps when you first dollied past
with your parents on the way home
from Uncle Stanley's funeral.

It's the strange, formidable, fun landmark
of the northwest side,
a focus to downtowners who blur over
even imagining blocks beyond Belmont & Western.

Elvis's kissin' cousin made it boy/girl, boy/girl
up the tower spiral against promises of red rainbows,
amongst silhouetted stories
in rear-lit windows next door.

The Leaning Tower of Touhy's
postcard appeal has kept me at bay from O'Hare,
the call of European destinations,
saving me cash, lost passports, missed connections.

Instead of Pisa's cathedral square
lies the Tower YMCA where no archbishop sleeps,

but serves as second home to divorced Mr. Chicagos
flexing muscle against our winter storms.

There are no post-Sunday-mass baptisms here,
but immersion swim class for babies who arrive
as modern pastiche of old worlds, who

Take one: breathe in, take two: submerge,
take three: arise as Chicagoans.

Louie Armstrong Painted Over Music Notes | *Adam Kress*

for Whitney

Louie Armstrong, Mr. Grey, circa 1984

You must love
    Like Louie Armstrong
Painted Over Music Notes
    Multidimensional
A textured installation piece
    Colorful and Soulful
Essence juxtaposed atop notes and lines
    Even your negative space has meaning
Like the music notes
    Despite their black and white
Shape connoting depth
    Inextricably intertwined
Like Satchmo's Trumpet
    Tied to his spirited rhyme
You are the feminine clef
    Keeping the notes in perfect time
You must love like
    Louie Armstrong painted over music notes

War Hole | *Maggie Westland*

Camouflage, Andy Warhol, 1986

If you want to be really ironic
take a couple of buckets of green and brown paint.
Take a couple of months to design just the right shades of gray
to add in to make all the squiggly lines interact on your page
which is made up of yards of compact dense fabric.
Make sure you display your creation in a prominent place.
Say your name is Andy and scrawl it in an equally prominent script.
Go away and pretend you are hiding.
Call your work *Camouflage*.

The Party | *Elizabeth Iannaci*

The Great Appear to Be Great Because We Ourselves Are Standing On Our Knees,
Valentina Egorovna & Viktor Konstantinovich Dhorokov, 1990

Okay. The guest list. Start with the famous: Stalin, Engels, Lenin, & Nadezhada Krupskaya. Maybe Trotsky, and Jack Reid. Ask Ché to come. By and by. Don't even THINK about inviting your boss. Leave the water balloons in the sink. You won't need them 'til later. Make sure you get rid of the engineers. They'll want to plan everything. The professors will just rest their small hands on their waistcoats, shake their beards, and make us all feel bad. So, let's not include them. The lawyers can come as long as they're quiet.

Don't let the logistics stop you. It's not complicated. Building the Panama Canal was complicated. Financing the rebellion, creating the Panamanian State.   The jungle. The Chagres River. The Yellow Fever. The malaria. Where to put all that dirt. You won't have to deal with any of that. Even if there is a mosquito or two. For food, you can let everyone eat cake.

Next, the invite. Choose a flashy graphic: something red and gold, perhaps a drawing of a tool or two. Then, a catchy slogan: *To each according to his greed.* Or: *Workers of the World keep right!* Use *Homeland* and *Mother Country* as often as you can—that'll spark interest with the regular folk. Once you get a good, rousing soundtrack you'll be home free. Remember, it sounded good to millions once. It'll still sound good to somebody, somewhere.

Now, put your tongue back in your mouth and hit "Send".

The Door for Love and Death | *Laurel Ann Bogen*

Doors, Tomaz Salamun, 1997

You push the shadow against the wall.
Open the door for love and death.
What rooms are rented there?

In the room of Exquisite Torture,
A woman watches her lover shave.

In the Room of Hopeless Romantic,
A man weeps before a portrait of Voltaire.

In the Room of Maternal Instinct,
The rose is embalmed.

In the Room of Amorous Adventure,
Both doors hide the tiger.

In the Room of My Life,
I give up one and love the other.

The Love Song of John Currin | *Noel Sloboda*

Honeymoon Nude, John Currin, 1998

Eve's skeleton sports a new suit,
tags torn out, riddled

with pinholes that release
the red ochre of uncertainty

and leave welts on the tongue.
In dusky predawn, the leer

of this other mother glistens
above an empty table, pinned

across scabby knees, making it
impossible to believe

the moon will not
feed itself to dawn.

Written in – and to be performed in – the style, or an approximation of the style, of Billy Collins | *Carolyn A. Martin*

After a description of a painting in the poem "Fishing on the Susquehanna in July,"
Billy Collins, 1998

Before the canvas, he brushes words.
Blue sky, red bandana, green boat, a thin pole
to fish the Susquehanna in July. Although,

he admits, he's never fished the Susquehanna;
perhaps, doesn't even like fish, July,
or red bandanas. I like Billy Collins. Actually,

not the man Billy Collins whom I've never met
except on YouTube with his balding head,
half-smile wit, and perfect words pointing

to themselves and, sometimes, to other things.
Nor the Billy Collins who can mesmerize an audience
with verbal acrobatics and flying twists

that make me want to cry, *How does he do this?*
in his drab suit-coat, no tie, and black glasses
he yo-yo's from podium to nose.

Rather, it's the poet who urges me to stand
at my window each sunrise – although the sun
doesn't really rise in my backyard.

It staggers through stands of Douglas fir,
fifty-five minutes after the newspaper says it should.
It hesitates, then shyly appears. Anyway,

as I was saying when sun popped in,
he wants me to ensure the neighbor's cat
has not made its presence smelt

in flower beds near my back fence;
and that someone is sitting at my table
waiting to listen to my poetry

over cereal bowls – or, in my house,
over spelt bread spread with coconut oil,
a healthy alternative to corn syrup

and other suspect things corporations hide
on well-stocked shelves. Which is not to say,
raw milk wouldn't sit on his table

near a bowl of organic berries cultivated
on the banks of the Susquehanna
by fishermen's wives, particularly

those who hate fishy red bandanas
and slime-green boats – while they wait
for men with thin poles to row a sunset home.

Beautiful Losers | *James Bell*

Beautiful Losers, Jack Vettriano, 2000

you have seen these three before
behind the walls of different houses
and know you have been one for a time

though flatter yourself over beauty
and its causes, how it can be lost -
while one nibbles her neck with faux love

an old encourager into even older folly
where everybody loses - this is after
the party - after false smiles and poses

the other, jacket on, sits lit cigarette
relaxes, looks on while confused emotions
party on to a next stage so near him

her low cut dress, his waistcoat and shirt
all stay on somewhere between a slapped face
and coitus - you know neither will be reached

she embraces herself as he holds her waist
from behind - the kiss on her neck
holds no passion, gives out as time passes

so these three sit or stand in a half
darkened room while the city outside
must be quiet and nothing more can be said

The falling man | *Fiona Curran*

The Falling Man, Richard Drew, 2001

has not landed yet.
His limbs are still questioning the sky
thirty floors on.
                         Clothes rent by velocity,
skin a flag flying the face,
voice sandpapered away
and the sound, the sound
the roar before the body breaks.

Accelerating into oblivion,
human debris raining all around
he makes a beautiful mark on the sky.
Nothing can catch him now,
wind whistling through the brain
chasing all coherent thought away,
everything he's ever lost or found
is compacted
                         filed in mid-air eternity:
rushing up as he rushes down
to fold like paper into the ground.

Two questions for anyone
thinking of doing it | *John Stewart Huffstot*

Untitled (ink on skin), anonymous, early 21st century

Saw a twenty-something woman with her tattoos this morning
counted nine but I bet
the skimpy top still hid a few
and she had pants of course (knee length)
when I say nine do not think
of symphony with nine movements
or tune with nine-part harmony for example
or nine-track studio mix
I actually speed wrote it on a napkin snatched from an empty table
      something Celtic-like wrapping most of an arm
      Yin-yang surrounding and invading navel surmounted by
            flaming death's head
            all inside a heart (counting this as one)
      dragon spread-winged across the whole small of her back
      a phrase, in Arabic I believe
      roses smothering backside of shoulder, they were red
      also red, winking infant devilish red devil with pitchfork
            on other shoulder backside
      some sort of coat of arms (a curly-cue shield with stuff,
            two lions, and Latin)
      Betty Boop
      massive lightning bolt on left ankle exterior (never saw
            the right but I'm thinking matched pair but I
            don't count the unseen supposition)
in fairness I also did not see an anchor extolling USN but recall the
top and pants
here's the thing
if one is good is nine nine times better?
yeah I guess it's her skin so I should just let her
still I wanted to speak up but didn't
excuse me Miss pain-in-the-retina eyeball noise
I'm getting no sensory reason or rhyme here
do you listen to nine songs all at the same time dear?

Paterno Statue with Football Players in Background | *Leland James*

Joe Paterno Statue, Angelo DiMaria, 2001

One might imagine
—once upon a time—
Joe's numero-uno finger
pointedly, up, up, up,
receiving sparks divine,
God's digit touching his:
an all-American Adam
of celebrity, pristine,
the touch *Sistine*, but then ....

A small plane flies overhead:
a banner tailing an artistic
afterthought; a fluttering addendum
to 9,000 pounds of bronze below,
"Take the statue down or we will"

Joe's sport coat flies bat-cape-like
behind: "No, Joker!" cries this
super hero to the circling plane,
"Here I stand! My boys
—dull shadows on the wall—
will lift me above a mere
assistant pedophile ...."

Go pink and black!
Students rally behind the icon,
with not a hint of irony, cursing
the sky. *Art* punts on CNN.

The work, itself, seen through the haze:
a yellowish prosaic claymation,
a histrionic abomination,
a bronze cartoon from the gitgo.

Go Joe. Go!

Bugger This for a
Game of Soldiers | *Ann Drysdale*

The Lord of the Rings film series, directed by Peter Jackson, 2001-2003

*The story has it that when the computer wizards fabricated
the battle scenes for Lord of the Rings, the Director decreed
that each figure should be programmed to act as an individual
and, during the first conflict, some of them ran away...*

Hiding in the enhanced hills of the antipodes
We are doing not too badly, all things considered.
We have each of us chosen to step outside the picture
And watch it dispassionately, without benefit of popcorn.

We happy few, we voluntary out-takes -
Virtually indestructible, having no substance -
Sought out our several ways into this haven.
Like Legionnaires, we do not discuss our reasons.

We are a small fistful of hand-knitted fictions,
With fellowship programmed digitally into our pixels;
Having been created utterly true to ourselves
We cannot now be false to one another.

And so we fadge, we Orcs, Elves, Wraiths and Rohirrim,
Carousing round the fire in a ring.

Woman and Apple | *Suzanne Lummis*

Woman and Apple, Rachael McCampbell, 2003

Viewer, I may seem exposed, or,
let's be blunt, naked—even so,
this story belongs to me.
Look to the Northeast, those coppery
brushstrokes, how they hint
at shadow and flesh, bent knee, foot
peddling forward—Man who Exits
the Scene as if pulled
toward what happens next.
But he's not the same man who arrived
from some whereabouts, blinking
in the changed light, straining
to decipher my form;
he's been re-configured, re-thought.
And something took place here, beyond
the frame of your knowing.
Note that my face conveys history,
the roil of slow-turning secrets,
while his form means only departure.
My feet languish in the spill
of heated snow, warmed-up rain,
seven degrees cooler than my skin.
This means something.
You regard yourself as intelligent—
explain it to yourself.
And you've mastered a bit of French:
Ceci n'est pas une pipe.
So of course there's no apple,
just the bare, see-through idea
of apple. But did you know it's a herring
(and slippery), a false lead?
In fact I'm dreaming of another fruit.
(Think autumn, crimson,
underworld. *It does not peel.*)
Meanwhile, in a painting nearby,

something's stopped—the small pump,
weight of a tongue tip, in a bird's chest.
The body falls, wing over
wing, searing a line through the air
only a bird's eye could see.
Dressed One, One Who Nods
and Moves On, did you imagine

    I'd reveal myself to *you?*

Empty Bed Gaston Street 2004 | *Florence Weinberger*

Bed on Gaston Street, Preston Russell, 2004

Scumbled sheets, chair, door, robe,
French windows, curtains of course, and outside, trees.
One side of the bed still taut, the wan sun might be tinder
for the man who sleeps alone.

Russell's filtered strokes stoke the wooden floor enough;
the bed's inhabitant had no need of slippers.
Sun's transit woke him (no clock in sight.)
He's left the robe hanging on the door like a poster.

We don't know who makes the bed; maybe after breakfast
she'll come back, prolong her nap.
Maybe bedding hides a doll rolled underneath, a Bible
or a letter still unwritten or unread, a stain we don't see.

Every humble house has, at dawn,
or following an afternoon tryst, an unmade bed,
a lingering light, a hint of heat.

De Young De Young | *Mira Martin-Parker*

The new De Young Museum in San Francisco, CA, Architects Jacques Herzog,
Pierre de Meuron and Fong and Chan, 2005

They kept Theibaud by the café with the large colored balls and
at the ticket counter cappuccinos were being served to a bronze
hole in the ground. The Helen Diller Family Court was so full
of stones and people dressed in black that the man checking
bags started playing the slit drum from Papua, New Guinea.
Thank God the place was open all night for Family Day festivities.
Numerous site-specific commissions and 45 years of master
prints brought Edwin Church to the upper level, where pixels
and a $5 exhibition fee applied. No worries, the Pool of
Enchantment was a burrowing sink by Warlukurlangu artists,
sponsored by Wells Fargo. There was much performing and
re-classifying to be had, and Catherine Wagner was heading for
Northern Territory, decked out in ferns and glass and light. The
Phyllis C. Wattis free triangular benches were accompanied by
thank you doors that opened wide for architecture and a sense
of place, and the entrance on the concourse level near the
Bernard and Barbra Osher wing had a very large safety pin
stuck in the ground. Which was fine, since no one was stranded
by the Nancy B. and Jake L. Hamon Tower observation floor
because there were several convenient Muni connections and a
spectacular dirt pile. Nan Tucker McEvoy's wing had a sculpture
garden with 5 easy ways to join, and for the hungry, Herzog & de
Meuron's multifacited destination hired Fong and Chan to serve
up a state-of-the-art landmark—one taking into consideration
the natural landscape, creating a particular kind of heaven.

To Die with Eyes Wide Open | *Stanley H. Barkan*

To Die with Eyes Wide Open, Adel Gorgy, 2006

Out of the depths
(inside the pyramids)
wide-open eyes
piercing
the supernal dark,
the enigma
of existence—
the last place—
captured here
in a face,
a portrait—
a portal into
the endless
mystery
where we have
come from,
where we are
going,
why we are
here.

Second Skin | *F.J. Bergmann*

Untitled, Benjamin Pierce, 2007

The problem with tattoos is,
you have to show some skin
for best effect. Knuckle-letters
on cold-stiffened fingers poking
out from your parka suffer badly
in comparison to snarling green
dragons wreathed in plumes of fire
that cover most of your glistening,
oiled, naked torso. What a pity that
most places require (at least) shorts!
But a shirt, you can wear all the time,
pretty much. What's not to like about
bright yellow single-needle tailoring
with arcane designs in black indelible
paint frothing and clawing over every
inch of buttercup-colored cloth? Even
the armpits flaunt the spoor of Art.
And if you go somewhere you can't
wear it, draped over your bedside
reading light, it would make
one hell of a lampshade.

Magnificat | *Mary Buchinger*

PixCell-Elk#2, Kohei Nawa, 2009

In a gallery in
Australia   I saw a grey and
honey-yellow elk covered in
thousands of glass bubbles
cupping patches of fur   a
circle of ear   hoof   snout
roughed-up horn.

The elk   inside dead
but shining.

The   glass
inhaled light   bent the
fluorescence to magnify like
Mary   for   Elizabeth   the
gorgeousness at the very
surface of the blank   and
terrible.

What   natural
shoulders bear   what
invisible resin   holds these
clear-seeing eyes   in place
you   wonder.

Mama | *Farida Samerkhanova*

The Red Maple Leaf, Rinat Haris, 2010

A so-loved-by-you maple leaf
Beautifully falling down onto the driveway
Mercilessly reminds me of the minute
When you gracefully cut off connections
With this disturbing world
On a very unexpectedly unhappy October day
Causing no trouble to anyone and
Leaving a train of precious exalted
Memories in my devastated soul

Tagger | *Gabrielle Mittelbach*

tagging on a garage, anonymous, 2010

My neighbor white washed his wall today.
While we slept, Pesci sprayed his name there in black.
I have seen his name on the freeway too.
Pesci, near the Culver off-ramp and over by 26th Street.
He's not artistic, but his lines are straight.
At least his mother can say he has good penmanship
and he probably hung upside-down off the overpass
to paint the one by Venice.
I think somewhere in the darkness, he shakes his aerosol can
and the bead inside hits metal and echoes in the hollowness.
What is it about that sound that reminds
us of our own hearts?
Somewhere in the darkness, I shake my aerosol cans too,
only they aren't cans. They are worries that rattle my gut.
They are thoughts that tap tap like water.
They are my ears as I try to hear my made-up name,
my Pesci, my Chaka, my Tuco, my Boon.
They are my rasps as I try to speak it
and I don't know how it represents me.
What does my name do?
It might as well be a number, it could be twelve,
I made it up. I paint the walls with my name,
my name, my made-up name.
I want everyone to see it on street signs,
on the road, in the bathroom stall.
Maybe it will mean something to someone.
Maybe someone will recognize their own name in it.
Maybe if we look deep enough, we all have the same made-up name.

White Crosses | *Jan Chronister*

Roadside Marker, Stephani Schaefer, 2010

They stand stiffly along highways
bookmarks in pages of miles
urging us to read
their stories.

A Wisconsin groom
leaves his bachelor party
relieves himself in the road, is struck
and killed by his best man's truck.

High school boys
in a car clattering with cans
hit a train
leave behind two teams
each one man short.

Even in the Everglades,
Joe Tigertail, son of a Seminole guide,
has his name in big black letters
on a cross of lath strips painted white,
end of a father's story.

Gynecology | *Eric Tuazon*

The Great Wall of Vagina, Jamie McCartney, 2011

She is not a simple woman, she tells me--
There is an embarrassing story, one
of her husband who is not like her.
They have gone and looked at a wall:
a wall of vagina. Different molds of vagina,
four hundred in all. Her husband,
unlike her, cannot bear to look.
He does not understand. "Why must
I look at these vaginas? How is this art?"
He asks. He leaves without her and,
later, she scolds him.
"It's art. It's supposed to be beautiful.
Don't you think I am beautiful?"
Later, she asks me,

"What is your poetry like?"
and I think, if I could, I would tell her,
but then there are things that happen,
like what happened to her husband.

I write and it starts with him,
her husband, who turns into pages
of her, his wife. I go on and on.
Details.
There are pages of her
hair, her toes, every part.
I stop to look over
what I have written.

Then her husband comes into a gallery,
and there is a detail on the wall.
At first, he does not see it, there is too much,
and then she points it out. "There I am," she says.
And he sees it---its shape and size, what he has
felt, what he has gone through, so different from

any other he has seen--- and then he does not.
It gets lost, in all of the other parts.
He does not understand where it has gone,
where it is going. He sees other men and me
looking for it and wonders what we are
going to do with it. The idea, it is nothing
beautiful, it is nothing he likes.

And, later, when he leaves
and the gallery is over,
I have been watching and
know where to find her.

Later,
I am finished and
there is a poem,
and in a gallery,
there is a wall
and someone walking away.

Marfa Gallery | *Peggy Trojan*

A visit to Dennis Dickinson's gallery, Exhibitions 2d, Marfa, Texas, 2011

In the old adobe,
Dennis shows one artist
on each wall.
Sure, bold, blacks and whites,
commanding you to look,
even study,
before moving on .
Pieces that do not want to share
space or your attention.
Graphite blocks polished to sheen,
velum paper layered with image,
prints, sculpture,
each an exclamation point.
Singular,
like scotch on the rocks.
Like the two a.m. train whistle.
Like last night's full moon
hanging low
in the navy black Texas sky.

I, Meaning You | *Brendan Constantine*

Inspired by one night's worth of books, music & television including Emily Dickinson,
Lord Byron, Chuck D, Allen Ginsberg, Sylvia Plath, Diane Di Prima, Caesar Vallejo,
The Nag Hammadi, Ellyn Maybe, Flavor Flav, Ice Cube, Dante Alighieri, Andrew Marvell,
Gwendolyn Brooks, Mindy Nettifee, Tupac Shakur, A.E. Housman, Robert Hayden,
Marie Howe, T.S.Eliot, Virgil, and The Evening News - 7:00 pm, September 17th 2012

The soul selects her own society
She walks in beauty like the night
But her brain s'being washed by an actor
                              —old woman of skulls—
This lady here's no kin
Of mine, yet kin she is:

what is that I cannot bear to say
?Hay golpes en la vida, tan fuertes... ¡Yo no sé!

The soul is a woman, the soul is always a woman

ৡৄৣ

There are people
            who wear their weather
            like perfume

Everyday they don't never come correct—
Though the heart be still as loving,
with a little bit of gold and a pager,
at my back I always hear
Time's winged chariot hurrying near;
I've stayed in the front yard all my life

ৡৄৣ

If you're trying to size me up, allow me to do it for you
In my mind I'm a blind man doin' time
And down in lovely muck I've lain, Happy till I woke again
I'd wake and hear the cold splintering, breaking
but I don't think there was a day like that for me

No! I am not Prince Hamlet, nor was meant to be;

The soul is a girl in love with her father
The father is a man who shot his daughter's computer
Birds are resuming for Him

Anonymous Rooms
with Automatons | *Neil Ellman*

Anonymous Rooms with Automatons, Pavel Zoubok, 2012

In each and every room
of my apartment house
anonymous automatic lives
anatomically correct
half human
half metal and plastic
transfixed by TV screens
realities not their own
reclining on soft sofas
sipping vodka by half-pints
smoking cigarettes
dropping ashes
that burn the skin
half alive
half asleep
dreaming of dinner
on aluminum plates
double-locked doors
grated windows
safety from
that other world
with no life other
than in four walls.

The Louisville Slugger Strikes the Broken Cup of Peace | *Peggy Dobreer*

after dual exhibits Baseball, and Ehren Tool's Cups of War,
Craft and Folk Art Museum, Los Angeles, 2012

Hey batter, batter. Hey batter.
Until spring of 1893 there was no
standard size for the baseball bat.
You could make one any length.
Experiment with knobs and wood.
Many a bat was tried and split.
Some cuts found too brittle to absorb
the force of a leather ball. Maple
and ash were determined best.

When the bases are loaded, squadrons
in place, the heat is on, dugout like
a foxhole. And now bats are regulated,
forty-two inches long, two and three
quarters diameter at the widest point.
War could be regulated like that? Simple
rules like a game of cups on sidewalk.
Watch the cup that covers the glass eye.
Don't take your baby blues off that cup.

The cup with the gas mask,
the cup with the bomb's blood,
the agent orange, the hello kit cup.

The cup that reads war is a racket,
the one where Mrs. Bush says,
Why do we have to hear about body bags
anyway? They're so unpleasant.

A cup of hand grenade, red clay of VietNam,
white bisque of dove, sic semper tyrannis.
How force intoxicates. The missile,
the sword, the skull and crossbones.
The rifle, the devil, the pawn. The
bullet, the cup. The bullet, the cup.
The bullet pierces the cup. The bullet
shatters the cup. The bullet, the dust,
the shattered cup.

Contributors

A.J. Huffman is a poet and freelance writer in Daytona Beach, Florida. She has previously published six collections of poetry all available on Amazon.com. She has also published her work in numerous national and international literary journals. Most recently, she has accepted the position as editor for four online poetry journals for Kind of a Hurricane Press (www.kindofahurricanepress.com). Find more about A.J. Huffman, including additional information and links to her work at facebook.com/amy.huffman.5 and twitter.com/poetess222

Ackroyd Jackson is 32 years old and lives in Surrey, UK. His work appears in places like *Ambit, Envoi, Poetry Salzburg Review,* and *14.*

Adam Kress is the author of two collections of poetry and numerous individual publications. In addition to his own writings, he is considered an expert on, and has a passion for the works of Pablo Neruda. He holds a master's in gender and legislative politics from Rockefeller College, an MPA from Cornell University and a dual bachelor's degree from Elmira College. Kress currently serves as Assistant Director of Communications and Semester in Washington for the Rockefeller College of Public Affairs and Policy, University at Albany-SUNY, where he is also a doctoral candidate in the Department of Political Science.

Alan Britt's interview at The Library of Congress for *The Poet and the Poem* (http://www.loc.gov/poetry/media/avfiles/poet-poem-alan-britt.mp3) aired on Pacifica Radio in January 2013. His interview with Minnesota Review is up at minnesotareview.wordpress.com . He read poems at the World Trade Center/Tribute WTC Visitor Center in Manhattan, New York City, April 2012. His recent books are *Alone with the Terrible Universe* (2011), *Greatest Hits* (2010), *Hurricane* (2010), *Vegetable Love* (2009), *Vermilion* (2006), *Infinite Days* (2003), *Amnesia Tango* (1998) and *Bodies of Lightning* (1995). Alan currently teaches English/Creative Writing at Towson University.

Alan Price is a London based poet. He has been published in such magazines as *Envoi, Orbis, The Interpreter's House, Obsessed with Pipework, The Delinquent and The Royal Shakespeare Company Website.* Alan's debut collection of poetry Outfoxing Hyenas was published by Indigo Dreams in 2012. Alan is also a scriptwriter. The trailer for his latest film *Pack of Pain* can be viewed online at IMDB. The film has won four international film festival awards.

Alan Wickes grew up in Northumberland, England. He studied History of Art and English Literature at Manchester and Open University. His work has appeared on both sides of the Atlantic, featuring in *Aesthetica, Znine, Worm, Loch Raven Review, The Chimera, Envoi, The Raintown Review* and *Soundzine*, as well as appearing as a 'spotlight poet' in *'The Hypertexts'*. His sonnets have won Ware Poets national competition twice, in 2004 and 2009. Cannon Poets awarded first prize to his poem *Parting Shots* in November 2006. In November 2007 his chapbook *Prospero at Breakfast* was published by Exot Books.

Ann Drysdale is a poet, non-fiction writer and journalist, born near Manchester, raised in London, married in Birmingham, ran a small holding and raised three children on the North York Moors and now lives half way up a mountain in South Wales. She was a journalist writing, among other things, the longest-running by-line column for the Yorkshire Evening Post. She's won many prizes for her writing and written several poetry and non-fiction books, including the two-part memoir *Three-three, two-two, five-six and Discussing Wittgenstein*, described by Professor Raymond Tallis as a 'masterpiece'.

April Salzano teaches college writing in Pennsylvania and is working on her first several collections of poetry and an autobiographical novel on raising a child with Autism. Her work has appeared in *Poetry Salzburg, Pyrokinection, Convergence, Ascent Aspirations, The Rainbow Rose, The Camel Saloon, The Applicant, The Mindful Word, Napalm and Novocain, Jellyfish Whispers, The South Townsville Micro Poetry Journal, The Weekender Magazine, Deadsnakes, Winemop, Daily Love, WIZ, Visceral Uterus, Crisis Chronicles* and is forthcoming in *Inclement, Poetry Quarterly, Decompression, Work to a Calm, Windmills* and *Bluestem*.

Benjamin Taylor Lally is the English Department Head at Burlington High School in Burlington, Massachusetts. His poetry has been published in The Formalist, ISPS, Winning Writers and 14 by 14.

Brendan Constantine is a poet based in Hollywood. His work has appeared in *FIELD, Ploughshares, Rattle, ZYZZYVA, the Los Angeles Review* and other journals. His most recent books are *Birthday Girl With Possum* (2011 Write Bloody Publishing) and *Calamity Joe* (2012 Red Hen Press). He teaches poetry at the Windward School and is an adjunct professor at Antioch University Los Angeles. He also conducts workshops for hospitals, foster homes, & with the Art of Elysium.

Brooke Dorn lives in Robinson, Illinois. She had a poem published in *The Anthology of Poetry by Young Americans* in 2002 and has written many more poems and a fictional novel since then.Brooke has a blog detailing her writing career at www.questinganagent.blogspot.com

Bruce Taylor is author of eight collections of poetry, including *The Longest You've Lived Anywhere: Poems New & Selected 2013,* and editor of eight anthologies, including, with Patti See, *Higher Learning: Reading and Writing About College.* His poetry has appeared in such places as *Able Muse, The Chicago Review, The Formalist, Light, The Nation, The New York Quarterly, Poetry, Rattle, Rosebud, Slow Trains* and *The Writers Almanac.*

After forty years in the academic and business worlds, **Carolyn Martin** is happily retired in Clackamas, OR where she gardens, writes, and participates in communities of creative colleagues. Her poems have appeared in publications such as *Naugatuck River Review, Becoming: What Makes A Woman, ninepatch,* and *On the Issues.* Her first collection, *Finding Compass,* was released by Queen of Wands Press, Portland, OR, 2011. Currently, she is president of VoiceCatcher, a nonprofit that connects women writers and artists in greater Portland, OR/Vancouver, WA.

Catherine Graham (UK) lives in Newcastle upon Tyne, England. She is an award-winning poet. Catherine's chapbook Signs (ID on Tyne Press) was one of Poetry Kit's five favourite books for 2011. Catherine's work has appeared in anthologies alongside internationally acclaimed poets including Robert Hass and Paul Muldoon in The Stony Thursday Book (ed. Ciaran O'Driscoll, Arts Office of Limerick City Council, 2009.) And with Sharon Olds, Bob Dylan and Maya Angelou in Soul Feathers (ed. Ronnie Goodyer and Annie Morgan, Indigo Dreams Publishing, 2011). Catherine's first full collection *Things I Will Put In My Mother's Pocket* is published by Indigo Dreams www.indigodreams.co.uk

Colovic Dusan has published 17 books of poetry: Promise, 1984; There is day, 1985; Tree of lougeval wood, 1986; Ancestor satisfied smile, 1987; Hunger of time, 1989; The first year, the first day, 1994; We must say, 1995; Talking about you, 1997; Language of corn, 2000; Track cleaned light, 2002; In icon of soul, 2005; Orasac road, 2007; Echo of infinity, 2008; The gates of light 2009; To the Sons of the Celestial Secret, 2010 and Milk of Language, 2011; and Inside sky 2012.

Consuelo Marshall graduated in 2011 with an MFA, Creative Writing from California State University, Long Beach. She was poetry editor for *ARTLIFE Magazine* and her poems appeared in *Zambomba*, 1998, *ArtLife*, 2004, *Verdad* 2008, *Spillway*, 2010, *RipRap* 2011, *Bank Heavy Press*, 2012 and *The PackingHouse Review*, 2012.

Cynthia Gallaher is the author of five other published poetry collections: *Earth Elegance, Swimmer's Prayer, Night Ribbons, and Private On Purpose and Omnivore Odes* (chapbooks). She is listed on the Chicago Public Library's "Top Ten Requested Chicago Poets." Gallaher holds a degree in the History of Art and Architecture from the University of Illinois at Chicago.

Dan Fitzgerald resides in Pontiac, Illinois. He studied English literature at Illinois State University, Normal, Illinois and worked a long time in the printing field until technology de-installed the job. He is currently employed in the meat department of local grocer. He has been published in *Poetalk, Nomads Choir, Writers' Journal*, and *The Advocate*.

Daniel Y. Harris is the author of *Hyperlinks of Anxiety* (Cervena Barva Press, 2013), *The New Arcana* (with John Amen, New York Quarterly Books, 2012), *Paul Celan and the Messiah's Broken Levered Tongue* (with Adam Shechter, Cervena Barva Press, 2010; picked by *The Jewish Forward* as one of the 5 most important Jewish poetry books of 2010) and *Unio Mystica* (Cross-Cultural Communications, 2009). He is a three-time Pushcart Prize nominee. Some of his poetry, experimental writing, art, and essays have been published in *Denver Quarterly, European Judaism, Exquisite Corpse and The New York Quarterly,* His website is www.danielyharris.com.

David Chorlton was born in Austria, grew up in England, and spent several years in Vienna before moving to Phoenix in1978. He pursued his visual art and had several shows as well as writing and publishing his poetry in magazines and collections, the latest of which is *The Devil's Sonata* from FutureCycle Press. Although he became ever more interested in the desert and its wildlife, the shadow side of Vienna emerges in his fiction and The Taste of Fog, which was published by Rain Mountain Press.

Deborah P. Kolodji is the moderator of the Southern California Haiku Study Group, which meets on the third Saturday of the month at the Pacific Asia Museum. A former president of the Science Fiction Poetry Association, she is also a member of the Haiku Society of America, the Haiku Poets of Northern California, and the Yuki Teikei Haiku Society of San Jose. Her poems, essays, and short stories have appeared in journals and webzines such as poeticdiversity, Rattle, THEMA, Strange Horizons, Frogpond, Tales of the Talisman, Modern Haiku, Star*Line, and the Magazine of Speculative Poetry. Her work has been anthologized in Chicken Soup for the Dieter's Soul, After Shocks, the Red Moon Anthology, and the Rhysling Anthology. She has published four chapbooks of poetry.

Desmond Kon Zhicheng-Mingdé has edited more than ten books and co-produced three audio books. These span the genres of ethnography, journalism, poetry, and creative nonfiction, several edited pro bono for non-profit organizations. Trained in publishing at Stanford, with a theology masters (world religions) from Harvard and fine arts masters (creative writing) from Notre Dame, he is the recipient of the PEN American Center Shorts Prize, Swale Life Poetry Prize, Cyclamens & Swords Poetry Prize, and Stepping Stones Nigeria Poetry Prize, among other awards. Desmond is an interdisciplinary artist, also working in clay. His commemorative pieces are housed in museums and private collections in India, the Netherlands, the UK and the US.

Don Mulcahy, born in Wales, is now a Canadian citizen living in Strathroy, Ontario, Canada. Following an academic career in dentistry, his poetry, prose, book reviews and opinion articles have appeared in dental journals, newspapers, *The HS Newsletter,* Wales (archived in The National Library of Wales), *The Prairie Journal, Matrix, Coffee House Poetry* (U.K.), *iota* (U.K.), *Verse Afire, fait accomplit, blood ink,*

Tower Poetry, the Antigonish Review, Vallum, the anthologies *Butterfly Thunder, Sounding the Seconds, Ascent Aspirations,* the *Voices Israel 2013 Poetry Anthology* and online at www.blueskiespoetry.ca, www.prairiejournal.org and www.magazine.utoronto.ca/writers-circle.

Doris Lueth Stengel born in North Dakota, a graduate of University of North Dakota, lives in Minnesota. A retired schoolteacher, concluding her career at an Alternative High School in Brainerd, Minnesota. She is Past President of the Heartland Poets, the League of Minnesota Poets and the National Federation of State Poetry Societies (NFSPS). She has poetry published in journals, magazines and anthologies including: *Encore, The Moccasin, Dust & Fire, Talking Stick, Lakes Country Journal, Her Voice, County Lines.* Her chapbook *Small Town Lines* was published by Finishing Line Press, Georgetown, Kentucky in July 2012.

Douglas Richardson was born in Duluth, Minnesota, and raised in Camarillo, California. He currently lives in Los Angeles, where he works as a proofreader and editor. Recent publication credits include *Straight Forward Poetry, The Nervous Breakdown, Misfits' Miscellany, Poetry Breakfast,* and the anthology *The Night Goes On All Night.*

Elizabeth Iannaci was born in New Haven, shares a birthday with Red China, Julie Andrews, Jimmy Carter and the anniversary of the day Roger Maris hit his 61st home run. Raised in Southern California, she's never been on a surfboard. She once hitchhiked across country with her then husband, on the way trading a bottle of Hai Karate aftershave for two ZagNut candy bars and a pack of Winston cigarettes. For a number of years Elizabeth made her living as a Marilyn Monroe impersonator. She earned an MFA in poetry, and writes letters on paper that are still delivered by humans.

Ellaraine Lockie is a widely published and awarded poet, nonfiction book author and essayist. Her recent work has been awarded Best Individual Collection from *Purple Patch* magazine in England, the San Gabriel Poetry Festival Chapbook Contest Prize and *The Aurorean's* Chapbook Pick. Forthcoming is her tenth chapbook, *Coffee House Confessions,* from Silver Birch Press. Ellaraine also teaches poetry workshops and serves as Poetry Editor for the lifestyles magazine, *Lilipoh.*

Eric Evans is a writer and musician from Buffalo, New York with stops in Portland, Oregon and Rochester, New York where he currently resides. His work has appeared in *Artvoice, decomP magazinE, Tangent Magazine, Posey, Xenith Magazine, Anobium Literary Magazine, Pemmican Press, Remark* and many other publications and anthologies. He has published seven full collections and three broadsides through his own small press, Ink Publications, in addition to a broadside through Lucid Moon Press. He is the editor of *The Bond Street Review* as well as the proud recipient of the 2009 Geva Theatre Center Summer Academy Snapple Fact Award.

Eric Lawson's work has appeared in several literary magazines including *The Houston Literary Review, Subtopian Magazine, Hennen's Observer, Falling Star Magazine,* and *The Bicycle Review.* He is the author of three poetry chapbooks and two humor collections. He resides in Los Angeles, California with an ornery sense of humor and an invisible dog named Sheckie.

Eric Tuazon is an LA native. He has published several poems and short stories, and has participated in several writers' workshops. He is currently working on a collection of poetry entitled, Happy Bivouac, set for release at the end of 2013.

F.J. Bergmann frequents Wisconsin and fibitz.com, writing poetry, science fiction and what falls between those worlds, functioning (so to speak) as the poetry editor of *Mobius: The Journal of Social Change* (mobiusmagazine.com) and the editor of *Star*Line* (sfpoetry.com/ starline.html), the journal of the Science Fiction Poetry Association.

Farida Samerkhanova lives in Toronto, Ontario, Canada Her letters to the editor appeared in the magazines Elle Canada, Canadian Stories and Canadian Immigrant. Her poems, short stories and essays were published by more than 40 literary journals in UK, Canada, USA and Turkey Farida has new work accepted for publication by De La Mancha, The Mellow Neurotics Magazine, Erbacce, Enhance Magazine, The Ambassador and Knobl Press My work is translated into Russian, Tatar and Serbian languages She is participating in a documentary film titled "Her Choice – Hijab and Beyond the Dress Code", which is currently in production.

Fern G.Z. Carr is a member of The League of Canadian Poets, lawyer and teacher. She composes poetry in five languages and has been published extensively world-wide from Finland to Mayotte Island (Mozambique Channel). A winner of national and international poetry contests, her poetry has been set to music by a Juno-nominated musician. Carr was recently featured online in the arts section of Canada's national newspaper, *The Globe* and *Mail*. She also has had the honor of having her poem, "I Am", chosen by the Parliamentary Poet Laureate as *Poem of the Month* for Canada. www.ferngzcarr.com

Fiona Curran is a Lecturer in Filmmaking at Kingston University and is a poet, sonic artist & filmmaker. She holds an M.A. in Creative Writing from the University of East Anglia. As a poet she has been published widely in the UK & Ireland and her first poetry collection *The Hail Mary Pass*, was published by Wreckingball Press. As a sonic artist (moniker 21% and in partnership as Curran & Gershon) she has presented sonic works at the Car Boot Art Fair and The Literary Kitchen. She has recently produced two experimental films "Clean" & "Allium" and is working towards a gallery show.

Florence Weinberger is the author of four poetry collections, *The Invisible Telling Its Shape, Breathing Like a Jew, Carnal Fragrance,* and, *Sacred Graffiti.* Twice nominated for a Pushcart Prize, her poetry has appeared in numerous literary magazines and anthologies, including *The Comstock Review, Antietam Review, The Literary Review, Solo, Rattle, River Styx, Spillway, Nimrod, Calyx, Another Chicago Magazine, The Prose-Poem Project, The Pedestal, Ellipsis, Poetry East* and *The Los Angeles Review.* She was born in New York City, educated at Hunter College, California State Northridge and UCLA, and has worked as a teacher, legal investigator and consumer advocate.

Gabrielle Mittelbach is a poet born and raised in Los Angeles, CA. She is a voracious reader and believes in writing every day even if it is only a sentence.

Gene Grabiner's poetry has appeared in; *Rosebud, Ilya's Honey, Blue Collar Review, J Journal, In Our Own Words* (ezine), *Earth's Daughters, HazMat Review,* and other journals and anthologies. He was a runner-up in the 2012 William Stafford Award Competition, has been featured at the Jackson Heights Poetry Festival, in New York City, has read at IFPOR in Toronto, and was a 2002 semi-finalist at the "Discover" / *The Nation* national poetry competition, Unterberg Poetry Center, also in New York City. Grabiner lives in buffalo, New York and is a SUNY Distinguished Service Professor Emeritus.

Gerald Locklin is Professor Emeritus of English at California State University, Long Beach, where he taught from 1965-2007, and continues as an occasional part-time lecturer. A profile based on a retirement event was broadcast on NPR. He is the author of over 150 books, chapbooks, and broadsides of poetry, fiction, and criticism, with over 4000 poems, stories, articles, reviews, and interviews published in periodicals. His work is frequently performed by Garrison Keillor on his Writer's Almanac daily Public Radio program, is archived on his website, and is included in all three of Mr. Keillor's *Good Poems* anthologies.

Graham Fulton lives in Scotland. His work has appeared in numerous publications, in both Europe and the USA, including *Ambit, Edinburgh Review, Gutter, Stand, Word Riot, Raintown Review* and *French Literary Review*. His collections include *Humouring the Iron Bar Man* (Polygon, 1990) *This* (Rebel Inc, 1993) *Knights of the Lower Floors* (Polygon, 1994) *Black Motel/The Man who Forgot How to* (Roncadora Press, 2010) *Open Plan* (Smokestack Books, 2011) *Full Scottish Breakfast* (Red Squirrel Press, 2011) and *The Zombie Poem* (Controlled Explosion Press, 2011). 4 new full-length collections are to be published by Roncadora, Red Squirrel, Smokestack and Salmon Poetry.

Helen Bar-Lev (www.helenbarlev.com), born in New York, 1942, living in Israel for 42 years, has had over 90 exhibitions of her landscapes, including 33 one-person shows. Her books include *Cyclamens and Swords and other poems about the land of Israel, The Muse in the Suitcase,* both with Johnmichael Simon, *In Moonlight the Sky Will Slide* with Katherine L. Gordon, and her latest collection, *Everything Today.* Helen is Senior Editor of Cyclamens and Swords Publishing and former Secretary of Voices Israel. The 2 painters who have most influenced her are Corot and Van Gogh (who admired Corot.)

Iris Dan grew up bilingually, in a German-speaking family in Romania. She has a M.A. in Romance Languages from the University of Bucharest. She has lived in Haifa since 1980. She is married, has a grown daughter and works (quite happily) as a translator from and into a number of languages. From her Babel Tower, she sees the Mediterranean. She is a member of Voices Israel and a Pushcart Prize nominee.

James Bell has published two poetry collections, "the just vanished place" (2008) and "fishing for beginners" (2010) both from tall-lighthouse. A Scot by birth he now lives in Brittany, with his wife and resident tabby, where he continues to make and publish poems and tend his garden.

Jan Chronister lives near Maple, Wisconsin and teaches English at a tribal/community college in Cloquet, Minnesota. Her chapbook *Target Practice* was published in 2009 by Parallel Press at the University of Wisconsin-Madison. Her work regularly appears in regional anthologies.

Jerry Quickley has been asked to contribute to a variety of books and publications, including *Spoken Word Revolution: Slam, Hip Hop, and the Voice of a New Generation* (Source Books), *Twilight of Empire: Responses to Occupation* (Perceval Press), and several others. Jerry also recently finished writing and producing the film project *Rise Again,* and can be seen in several documentaries. He has collaborated with artists as diverse as Dee Dee Ramone, Philip Glass, Tom Morello, Viggo Mortensen, and Mos DEF. He has also been a Stanford University Visiting Fellow.

Jim Bennett lives is the author of 71 books, including books for children, books of poetry and many technical titles on transport and examinations. He taught Creative Writing at the University of Liverpool and other Universities. He has won many awards for his writing and performance including 3 DADAFest awards and is managing editor of www.poetrykit.org one of the world's most successful internet sites for poets. His latest book of poetry is "The Cartographer / Heswall" see www.indigodreamsbookshop.com/jim-bennett

John Huffstot is an American who married a Portuguese lady in 1984 and relocated to her home country, where they added three to the family over the years. He teaches language and communication at the business school of the *Universidade Nova de Lisboa.* Every summer finds him at the bay of *São Martinho do Porto,* where the artwork that inspired *"Two questions for anyone..."* plodded by in the sand, leaving a trail of impressions, indeed.

Johnmichael Simon was born in Northampton, England. After World War 2 he moved to South Africa with his family. He has lived in Israel since 1963. Today Johnmichael lives in Metulla with his partner Helen Bar-Lev, artist and poet. Since retiring from his technical writing career he has published four solo books of poems and two collaborations with Helen. He has been awarded numerous prizes and honorable mentions and is published widely. Johnmichael is the chief editor of *Cyclamens and Swords* publishing www.cyclamensandswords.com and editor of the *Voices Israel Group of Poets in English* annual anthology www.voicesisrael.com .

Kath Abela Wilson has been writing poetry incessantly since the age of five. She is the creator and leader of the band of "Poets on Site," a performance group of poets collaborating with dancers, musicians, artists and scientists on site of their inspirations. Poets on Site has produced 30 books and performances at museums, galleries and gardens in Southern California. She is also an artist, jeweler, singer, percussionist, and dancer and host the Caltech Red Door Poets, "the most dynamic poetry workshop in the scientific world".

Kathleen Krueger is a full time freelance writer and poet from Brainerd, Minnesota. Her intuitive, feelings-based personality strongly influences her creative writing, but is especially evident in her poetry, her first love, when it comes to crafting with words. She is a regular contributor to HerLife Magazine, among other print and online publications and may be contacted through her website at kmkrueger.net

Kenneth Pobo won the 2011 qarrtsiluni chapbook contest for *Ice And Gaywings*. Forthcoming from Finishing Line Press is *Save My Place*.

Kevin Cornwall earned a degree in cultural anthropology (UCSC) with a thesis on how the social structures of humans mirror the structure of their mythologies. He subsequently studied dream theory and modern art. After rewarding careers as a longevity consultant and jazz musician, he currently works designing digital interfaces -- melding form, function, and content. He lives in San Diego, CA with his Russian wife and two darling daughters.

Laurel Ann Bogen is the author of ten books of poetry and short fiction. In 2014 Red Hen Press will publish her New and Selected Poems. A native of Los Angeles, she teaches in the Writers' Program at UCLA Extension where she received the Outstanding Instructor of the Year award in 2008.

Leland James was an International Publication Prize winner in the *Atlanta Review* 2011 International Poetry Competition, the winner of the Portland Pen Poetry Contest and the Writers' Forum Short Poem contest, and runner up for the Fish International Poetry Prize. He received the Franklin-Christoph Merit Award for Poetry in 2008. His poems have been published in eight countries in many periodicals and anthologies, including, *The South Carolina Review, New Millennium Writers, Vallum, Orbis, Magma,* and *Osprey, Scotland's international journal of literature; the 2008 Fish Anthology: Harlem River Blues* and *Voices Israel 2009.*

Letitia Minnick's poetry has been published in several academic literary magazines as well as her newsletter-turned-blog: The Rogue Nun. She enjoys stumbling on new poets and poetic forms and styles and finds as much satisfaction in encouraging others to share their art as she does when sharing her own.

M.A. Griffiths (1947-2009) was a British poet of English and Welsh heritage. From 2001 to 2008, Griffiths was a prolific participant in online poetry workshops, where she was known as grasshopper, Margaret, or Maz. She also edited the respected e-zine *~the (poetry) WORM~* from 2003 to 2008. Griffiths suffered for many years from a stomach ailment which eventually proved fatal. An international task force of her fans compiled the posthumous collection *Grasshopper: The Poetry of M.A. Griffiths* (Arrowhead Press, 2011) with the permission of her estate. Work is underway on a selected volume.

M.J.Iuppa lives on a small farm near the shores of Lake Ontario. Her most recent poems have appeared in *Poetry East, The Chariton Review, Tar River Poetry, Blueline, The Prose Poem Project,* and *The Centrifugal Eye,* among others. Recent chapbook is *As the Crows Flies* (Foothills Publishing, 2008) and second full length collection, *Within Reach,* (Cherry Grove Collections, 2010); Forthcoming prose chapbook *Between Worlds* (Foothills Publishing) She is Writer-in-Residence and Director of the Visual and Performing Arts Minor program at St. John Fisher College, Rochester, NY.

Maggie Westland, a lover of all things verbally musical, especially enjoys poetry as performance. She has been published in poetry anthologies, British and American literary magazines, and on-line podcasts. Maggie recently received third place in the Poetry Super Highway Contest, and 1st prize for ekphrastic poetry in the City of Ventura's Art Tales competition. A featured reader at various venues in Southern California, her work can also be seen on YouTube. Google *Maggie Westland* to find more of her poems.

Mantz Yorke is a retired teacher and researcher living in Manchester, England. He has worked for more than two decades with faculty teaching Art & Design in higher education.

Marie Lecrivain is a writer, editor, and photographer who resides in Los Angeles. She is the editor/publisher of *poeticdiversity: the litzine of Los Angeles.* Her work has appeared in various online/print journals, including *Haibun Today, Heavy Hands Ink, Illumen, The Los Angeles Review, Poetry Salzburg Review,* and others. Her newest poetry collection, *Love Poems... Yes... REALLY... Love Poems,* is forthcoming from Sybaritic Press. Her previous collections: *Bitchess* (copyright 2011 Sybaritic Press); *Antebelllum Messiah* (copyright 2009 Sybaritic Press), and *Nihilistic Foibles* (copyright 2005 Sybaritic Press), are available through Amazon.com.

Martin Bennett's poem collection - 'Loose Watches' - was published by University of Salzburg Press, and last year a pamphlet – 'Unlike the Jungle Pheasant' – was published by Red Squirrel Press. He has had three stories read of BBC World Service and other work appear in 'Lines Review', 'Chapman', 'Lines Review', 'Poetry Ireland Review', 'Stand', and 'Modern Poetry in Translation'. He lives in Rome where he teaches and proofreads at the University of Tor Vergata.

Mary Buchinger's poems have appeared in *AGNI, Booth, Pank, RUNES: A Literary Review, Slice, The Massachusetts Review, Versal,* and other journals; she was the recipient of New England Poetry Club's Daniel Varoujan and Firman Houghton Awards. Her collection, *Roomful of Sparrows,* was a semi-finalist in the New Women's Voices Series. She is Associate Professor of English and Communication Studies at the Massachusetts College of Pharmacy and Health Sciences in Boston.

Mary Harwell Sayler began drawing faces and writing poems as a child and, as an adult, placed a few photographs and about 1500 poems, devotionals, and children's stories in a variety of publications. Her 24 traditionally published books finally included all genres in 2012 when Hiraeth Press published her first full-length poetry book, *Living in the Nature Poem.* She also works with other poets and provides writing resources on her website – www.marysayler.com.

Maryann Corbett is the author of two books: *Breath Control* (David Robert Books) and *Credo for the Checkout Line in Winter* (forthcoming from Able Muse Press). She has been a winner of the Willis Barnstone Translation Prize and a finalist for the Morton Marr prize, the *Best of the Net* anthology, and the Able Muse Book Prize. Her poems, essays, and translations have appeared in many journals in print and online, such as *Atlanta Review, River Styx, Subtropics,* and *32 Poems,* and in a number of anthologies. She lives in St. Paul and works for the Minnesota Legislature.

Michael Virga, B.A. in English from Birmingham-Southern College, has been about Poetry circa 1987, but Poetry has been with him since conception. A bohemian cyber-poet, from Red Mountain (English Village), he contributes poetry on-line, in print, & on air. "I experienced the exhibition *Norman Rockwell's America* at the Birmingham Museum of Art where I am a Junior Patron member, and former touring docent; and, since the mic was first opened in 2009 for *BMA Speaks,* I continue as a dedicated reader for this museum series which encourages poetry prompted by the BMA's collection & visiting exhibitions, but welcomes all poetries."

Mick Moss. 59. Liverpool UK. Writer: poetry, prose, screenplays. Artist, musician. Published internationally, in print and on-line. Topped the internet music charts. Seeking outlets for new comedy material.

Mira Martin-Parker recently completed an MFA in creative writing at San Francisco State University. Her work has appeared in various publications, including the *Istanbul Literary Review, North Dakota Quarterly, Mythium,* and *Zyzzyva.*

Neal Whitman splits his time between Western and Japanese form poetry. He writes to be read – north of 600 poems have been published. His 2013 poetry prizes include the Blaze Memorial Award, Thief River Falls 2nd place, *Diogen Pro Kultura Magazin* (Serbia) Spring Haiku 3rd place and honorable mention, California Federation of Chaparral Poets honorable mention, and Ito En Haiku Grand Prix (Japan) semifinalist. Neal and his wife, Elaine, have published several haiga in newspapers, magazines, and journals: his haiku combined with her photography.

Twice nominated for Best of the Net, **Neil Ellman** lives and writes in New Jersey. Among his numerous published poems, more than 400 ekphrastic pieces based on works of modern and contemporary art appear in print and online journals, anthologies, broadsides and chapbooks throughout the world, from the United Kingdom to Australia, and from Ireland to the Philippines.

Noel Sloboda's work has recently appeared or is forthcoming in *Rattle, Modern Language Studies, Harpur Palate,* and *Kestrel.* He is the author of the poetry collection *Shell Games* (2008) as well as several chapbooks, most recently *Circle Straight Back* (Červená Barva Press, 2012). Sloboda has also published a book about Edith Wharton and Gertrude Stein. He teaches at Penn State York and serves as dramaturg for the Harrisburg Shakespeare Company.

Paula McKay lives and writes in Sydney. She is convenor of one of that city's finest group of writers 'The Walter Street Poets'. Her first collection of Poetry 'Travelling Incognito' was published by Five Islands Press in 1993. Her latest collection 'Why Policemen Stopped Flying' was published in December 2012 by Ginninderra Press.

Peggy Dobreer is a Los Angeles based poet, educator, and Yoga enthusiast. Her first book of poetry, *In The Lake of Your Bones* was published by Moon Tide Press, March 2012. Her work has been published in journals, such as Poemeleon, Malpais Review, The San Pedro River Review, and Yoga Magazine. She is co-author of *64 Ways to Practice Nonviolence: A Curriculum and Resource Guide,* ProEd, Inc., 2008.

Peggy Trojan retired from teaching English and Art to the north woods of Wisconsin where she and her husband built their own house next to a trout creek. A member of Wisconsin Fellowship of Poets, she has been published, among others, in *Dust and Fire, Talking Stick, Echoes, Verse Wisconsin, Wilda Morris Poetry Challenge,* and *Wisconsin Fellowship calendars.*

Perie Longo, Poet Laureate of Santa Barbara, California (2007-2009), has published three books of poetry: *Milking The Earth, The Privacy Of Wind,* and *With Nothing Behind But Sky: a journey through grief.* Her work has appeared in journals including *Askew, Atlanta Review, Connecticut Review, International Poetry Review, Nimrod, Paterson Literary Review, Poet Lore, Prairie Schooner, Rattle, South Carolina Review* and others. She teaches poetry for the Santa Barbara Writers Conference, California-Poets-in-the-Schools, and privately. As a psychotherapist, she integrates poetry for healing.

Peter Branson has been published in Britain, USA, Canada, Ireland, Australasia and South Africa, including *Acumen, Agenda, Ambit, Anon, Envoi, London Magazine, Warwick Review, Iota, Frogmore Papers, Crannog, Columbia Review, Able Muse, Barnwood* and *Other Poetry.* His first book came out in 2008, a second in 2010 (Caparison Press); more recently a pamphlet was issued by 'Silkworms Ink'. He has won prizes in recent years, a 'highly commended' in the 'Petra Kenny', firsts in the 'Grace Dieu' and 'Envoi' and a special commendation in the 2012 Wigtown. His latest book, *Red Hill, Selected Poems*, was published recently by Lapwing.

Phil Howard is a local authority worker who would like to see poetry restored as an art form which can be appreciated by all through relevant and accessible work that tackles compelling subject matter. Some of his newer poetry has been published in recent editions of *Snakeskin, Streetcake, Decanto, The Recusant* and *Prole.* He has also published a new collection - *Inside, Out and Beyond* - for Kindle.

Robert Wynne earned his MFA in Creative Writing from Antioch University. A former co-editor of Cider Press Review, he has published 6 chapbooks, and 3 full-length books of poetry, the most recent being "Self-Portrait as Odysseus," published in 2011 by Tebot Bach Press. He's won numerous prizes, and his poetry has appeared in magazines and anthologies throughout North America. He lives in Burleson, Texas with his wife, daughter and 4 rambunctious dogs. His online home is www.rwynne.com.

Ron. Lavalette lives in the very northeastern corner of Vermont, land of the fur-bearing lake trout and the bilingual stop sign. He has been widely published, in both pixel and print media. He's not quite dead yet. A reasonable sample of his work can be seen at: EGGS OVER TOKYO (eggsovertokyo.blogspot.com)

Rosalee Thompson's has always loved language. It all started with reciting The Angel of God prayer, when she was 3. She graduated from high school majoring in nothing but being unconventional. She has been published in over 80 literary magazines. Her world is colorful, beautiful and full of sacred secrets of the senses.

Salvatore Difalco resides in Toronto where he works as an Italian translator. His poems have been published in journals across Canada, Great Britain and the US.

Simon Jackson lives in Cairo. He has been a journalist, teacher, musician and director of Living Arts Space Theatre Company. His poetry is published internationally and translated into several languages. He has had more than twenty plays performed and won several awards including British Gas Young Playwright of the Year, The Grace Dieux Writers' Prize 2009 and 2012 and The Writers Bureau Poetry Award 2010. He has made videos for musicians including Billy Bragg and his series of short films based on Scottish poems have been used by the BBC and shown in Film Festivals around the world.

Simon Peter Eggertsen was born in Kansas, raised in Utah, schooled in Virginia and England. He has degrees in literature, language and law (BYU, Virginia, Queens' College, Cambridge). His verses have appeared in *Nimrod, Vallum* (Canada), *Atlanta Review, New Millennium Writings, Dialogue, and Weber: The Contemporary West.* He recently won the Irreantum Poetry Prize, has been a finalist for the Pablo Neruda Prize in Poetry (Nimrod), awarded an International Publishing Prize (Atlanta Review), and had two honorable mentions among the New Millennium Writing Awards #29. His work is anthologized in *Fire in the Pasture* and *Animal Doctors, Animal Companions.*

Sonja Smolec is a well known author of children books, giving numerous presentations and readings around her native country – Croatia. Sonja is also a member of several local organizations supporting art in all its forms as well as a member of the Croatian Society of Writers for Children and Youth. Being a prolific author she tries her hand in a variety of styles - poetry, mystery, novels, and

English poetry. With her short story «Night Howl» she won the prestigious international prize in a writing competition organized by "El Museo De La Palabra", year 2012, (Museum of Words), Spain.

Stanley H. Barkan is the editor/publisher of Cross-Cultural Communications that has, to date, produced some 400 titles in 50 different languages. His own work has been published in 15 collections. His latest are, *Strange Seasons*, a poetry and photographic collaboration with Russian artist, Mark Polyakov (2007) and *ABC of Fruits and Vegetables* (2012), poems from apple to zucchini with complementary drawings by his daughter, Mia Barkan (both-Sofia, Bulgaria: AngoBoy). He was the 1991 New York City's Poetry Teacher of the Year and the 1996 winner of the Poor Richard's Award, "The Best of the Small Presses."

Steve Ely lives in West Yorkshire in the United Kingdom.

Suzanne Lummis' publications, recent or forthcoming, include poems in *Hotel Amerika,* the debut issue of Christopher Buckley's new magazine, *Miramar,* in *Solo Novo*, a defining essay on the poem noir in *Malpais Review,* for which she is the California correspondent, and a book, *The Poetry Mystique: Inside the Contemporary Poetry Workshop,* from Duede Press. He next poetry collection will be published by Red Hen.

Timothy Charles Anderson lives in Southern Ontario. He is the author of *Hemp Poetic*, and *Funtimes the Snail*, a musical storybook for kids. His poetry is featured in the short film, *Orbit*, directed by Shunsuke Teshima. As a Personal Historian with Houseboat Memoirs, Timothy helps families record and preserve their life stories.

Tracy Davidson lives in Warwickshire, England, and enjoys writing poetry and flash fiction. Her work has appeared in various journals and anthologies including: *Atlas Poetica, Modern Haiku, Simply Haiku, Roundyhouse, The Right Eyed Deer, Mslexia* and *A Hundred Gourds*.

Wislawa Szymborska was born in 1923 in Bnin, a small town in Western Poland. Her family moved to Krakow in 1931 where she lived most of her life. She is the author of more than fifteen books of poetry and in 1996, she won the Nobel Prize in Literature. Her other awards include the Polish Pen Club prize, an Honorary Doctorate from Adam Mickiewicz University, the Herder Prize and The Goethe Prize. Wislawa Szymborska died on February 1, 2012 at the age of 88.

Acknowledgements

Janus by Iris Dan originally appeared in *Cyclamens and Swords* (November, 2012).

To Bellini by F.J. Bergmann originally appeared in *Tales of the Unanticipated.*

Last Supper by Doris Lueth Stengel originally appeared in *Encore – Prize Poems of the National Federation of State Poetry Societies.* (2008)

Mona Lisa Smiles by Dan Fitzgerald originally appeared in *Nerve Cowboy.* (Spring 2010)

Mona Lisa and David by Johnmichael Simon originally appeared in *Bordwinot.* (Cyclamens and Swords Publications, 2007)

Retrospect by Peter Branson originally appeared in his book *Red Hill, Selected Poems 2000-2012.* (Lapwing Publications, May, 2013)

Frans Hals: Portrait of a Woman by Gerald Locklin originally appeared in *The Mas Tequila Review* (Issue #4, Spring 2012) and along with the poem *Frans Hals: Boy with Lute,* subsequently in his book *Deep Meanings: New and Selected Poems 2008-2013.* (Presa Press, 2013)

Working Late by Phil Howard originally appeared in *Angle.* (Volume 2 - Issue 1, Spring/Summer 2013)

An earlier version of the poem *Lisa Gherardini Might Be Pregnant* by Simon Peter Eggertsen appeared under another title in *New Millennium Writings.* (Vol. 20, 2011)

Guardroom with the Deliverance of Saint Peter by Maryann Corbett originally appeared in *River Styx* (Spring 2009) and then in her book *Breath Control.* (2012)

Ode to Velázquez by Alan Britt originally appeared in *The Gothic: New Jersey City University's Alumni Magazine* and *Parabola Dreams: Poems* by Silvia Scheibli and *Alan Britt.* (The Bitter Oleander Press, 2013).

142

The Bath by Ellaraine Lockie originally appeared in *Taproot Literary Review*.

Magritte's Lovers by Eric Evans originally appeared in the book The *Anatomy of a Cratedigger* by Eric Evans. (Ink Publications, 2010)

Untitled by Paul Klee by Ellaraine Lockie originally appeared in *Ibbetson Street*.

The Firing Squad by Johnmichael Simon originally appeared in *Phyrrs, Hierwals and Bouldergeists.* (Assume Nothing Press, 2008)

Poem Inspired by Andrew Wyeth's The Revenant by Marie Lecrivain originally appeared in *Voices, Visions and Verses: Anthology for the New Britain Museum of American Art.* (2012 Exiles Press)

Dali Rage by Graham Fulton originally appeared in the collection *Full Scottish Breakfast.* (Red Squirrel Press, 2011)

Tracks by Donald Mulcahy originally appeared in *iota Literary Journal.* (Vol. 75, 2006)

A Last Hurrah by David Chorlton originally appeared in *Minotaur*.

A Time Comes When You No Longer Think It by M.J. Iuppa originally appeared in *The Montucky Review*.

Cows by Simon Jackson originally appeared in *Fragile Cargo* by Simon Jackson. (BeWrite Books, 2011)

Louie Armstrong Painted Over Music Notes by Adam Kress originally appeared in *Forword Magazine.* (Fall 2007 Edition).

The Love Song of John Currin by Noel Sloboda originally appeared in *EAPSU Online* (2011) and in *Luvah: Journal of the Creative Imagination.* (2012)

Written in – and to be performed in – the style, or an approximation of the style, of Billy Collins by Carolyn A. Martin originally appeared in her book *Finding Compass.* (Portland, Oregon: Queen of Wands Press, 2011)

Bugger This for a Game of Soldiers by Ann Drysdale originally appeared in *Quaintness and Other Offences.* (Cinnamon Press, 2009)

De Young De Young by Mira Martin-Parker originally appeared in *Zyzzyva,* Vol. XXII, No.1 (Spring 2006)

To Die with Eyes Wide Open by Stanley H. Barkan originally appeared in *Paterson Literary Review* (#40, 2012-2013), edited by Maria Mazziotti Gillan and in the Cross-Cultural Communications Broadside Series.

Mama by Farida Samerkhanova originally appeared on the Poetry Super Highway. (February, 2011)

Tagger by Gabrielle Mittelbach originally appeared in *Heard Magazine.* (www.heardmagazine.com - 2013)

White Crosses by Jan Chronister originally appeared in *Fog and Woodsmoke.* (Lost Hills Books, 2010)

More poetry from Ain't Got No Press

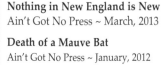

Nothing in New England is New
Ain't Got No Press ~ March, 2013

Death of a Mauve Bat
Ain't Got No Press ~ January, 2012

The Night Goes On All Night
Noir Inspired Poetry (edited by Rick Lupert)
Ain't Got No Press ~ November, 2011

Sinzibuckwud!
Ain't Got No Press ~ January, 2011

We Put Things In Our Mouths
Ain't Got No Press ~ January, 2010

A Poet's Haggadah (edited by Rick Lupert)
Ain't Got No Press ~ April, 2008

A Man With No Teeth
Serves Us Breakfast
Ain't Got No Press ~ May, 2007

I'd Like to Bake Your Goods
Ain't Got No Press ~ January, 2006

Stolen Mummies
Ain't Got No Press ~ February, 2003

Brendan Constantine is
My Kind of Town
Inevitable Press ~ September, 2001

Up Liberty's Skirt
Cassowary Press ~ March, 2001

Feeding Holy Cats
Cassowary Press ~ May, 2000

I'm a Jew, Are You?
Cassowary Press ~ May, 2000

Mowing Fargo
Sacred Beverage Press ~ December, 1998

Lizard King of the Laundromat
The Inevitable Press ~ February, 1998

I Am My Own Orange County
Ain't Got No Press ~ May, 1997

Paris: It's The Cheese
Ain't Got No Press ~ May, 1996

For more information:
http://PoetrySuperHighway.com/

26390430R00083

Made in the USA
Middletown, DE
27 November 2015